Queen Elizabeth

THE CROWELL HISTORICAL CLASSICS SERIES

UNDER THE EDITORSHIP OF *Herman Ausubel*

Queen Elizabeth by Mandell Creighton
WITH AN INTRODUCTION BY G. R. ELTON

Lord Beaconsfield by Georg Brandes
WITH AN INTRODUCTION BY SALO W. BARON

William Stubbs on the English Constitution
EDITED BY NORMAN F. CANTOR

Impressions of Russia by Georg Brandes
WITH AN INTRODUCTION BY RICHARD PIPES

IN PREPARATION

Americans of 1776 by James Schouler
WITH AN INTRODUCTION BY RICHARD B. MORRIS

The First Two Stuarts and the Puritan Revolution
by Samuel R. Gardiner
WITH AN INTRODUCTION BY WILLSON COATES

Hume by Thomas Henry Huxley
WITH AN INTRODUCTION BY ALBERT HOFSTADTER

Life of Andrew Jackson by William Cobbett
WITH AN INTRODUCTION BY MARCUS CUNLIFFE

ক্টিও ক্টিও ক্টিওঞ ঞিও ঞিও

Queen Elizabeth

BY Mandell Creighton

ক্টিও ক্টিও ক্টিওঞ ঞিও ঞিও

WITH AN INTRODUCTION
BY G. R. Elton

THOMAS Y. CROWELL COMPANY

Established 1834   New York

INTRODUCTION

↪§Queen Elizabeth, of Blessed Memory, ruled over her people for forty-five years, about half as long again as most of them had any cause to expect to live. When she herself died, nearly seventy years old, there were very few alive who could even recall that another sovereign had ever sat on the throne of England. And though towards the end she had been not only old but also somewhat out of touch with the attitudes and ambitions of a new generation, she retained to the last the love and worship of a nation accustomed to a monarchy clothed in the splendour of divine right but also embodied in palpably real people. Whatever else the Tudors may have been, they were aggressively alive, sculpted in the round, formidable personalities of the kind that create living legends in their own lifetime and do not lose their vitality even in death. The Queen's long reign accomplished the promise of her father's rule; the age of Elizabeth is rightly regarded, not only by historians but also in the popular memory, as a time of greatness breeding greater things still than it actually witnessed.

It is thus a little surprising that good biographies of Elizabeth should be so few in number. Here is a figure of history about whom it is easy to discover plenty of personal facts, known in detail from early childhood, heavily documented through sixty-nine years. Character is revealed in action, sayings, and writings. The interest of both person and period is undoubted and has never ceased. And if there are uncertainties, if the Queen could be an enigma to the observer, surely this should only stimulate the biographer and relieve him from feeling that the work has been done. Yet there are only two lives of Queen Elizabeth worthy of attention, both admittedly excellent: J. E. Neale's, published in 1934, which would now be generally regarded as the standard work, and this present book which first appeared in 1896 and still retains independent value after a time as long as the great Queen's own life. Neale's book owes its eminence to the employment of a professional historian's equipment, allied to literary skills of a high order; it embodies the research and understanding of a whole generation unknown to Creighton and benefits from solid interests in government and society alien to him. If in the opinion of those qualified to judge it has never-theless not succeeded in relegating Creighton's book to oblivion, this is in part because good studies of Elizabeth are so few, but in greater part because the bishop of London brought to his work special qualities which give a distinct and distinguished air to his life of Elizabeth.

Mandell Creighton was born on July 3rd, 1843, the son of a master carpenter of Carlisle in Cumberland.[1] He made his way by his brain. Educated at Durham Grammar School and Merton College, Oxford, he obtained a first class in Greats and, after only six months' study, a good second class in the honours school of law and history. Even before he took his degree he had been elected a Fellow of his College, and there he re-mained for nine years as the most influential of the tutors. Mar-riage in 1872 was followed by ordination in 1873, and in 1875 he decided to leave Oxford in order to vary his experience. His life as parson of Embleton in Northumberland was both pleasant and successful, and his duties left him time to begin his career as an historian. He had resolved to write the history of the Papacy from the Great Schism in 1377 to the Sack of Rome in 1527, and the first two of the work's ultimately six volumes were published when the Dixie chair of ecclesiastical history, founded

---

[1] For Creighton's life and person see *Dictionary of National Biography; Life and Letters of Mandell Creighton*, by his Wife (2 vols.; London, 1904); and W. G. Fallows, *Mandell Creighton and the English Church* (London, 1964).

at Cambridge two years before, came to be filled in 1884. Creighton's fame assured him of the appointment which he held, writing and teaching with vigour and success, for six years. In 1886 he joined with others in the foundation of the *English Historical Review*, became its first editor, and set standards both of content and typography which have altered little since.[2] In 1890, the world once more made its demands on one who at heart preferred the academic existence, and he obeyed the call to become bishop of Peterborough. From there he was in 1897 translated to the see of London, which at the time was convulsed by the ritualistic controversy provoked by Anglo-Catholic innovators and nourished by their bigotedly low Protestant opponents. Creighton here found a new opportunity for his great energy and his striking ability to use every minute of the day. However, overwork inflicted an ill-treated ulcer upon him, and he died, after a severe haemorrhage, in 1901, before the move to Canterbury, confidently predicted for him, could come his way.

In person, Creighton was tall, slender, with a big nose, long reddish beard, bald head, and formidable air. His mind exemplified the qualities commonly associated with men from the north country. He was plain, downright, determined, and though he quite liked the pomp and majesty of a bishop, he was entirely devoid of pretence and saw through himself as well as through others. In the solemn setting of the late-Victorian Church, his sardonic wit and a liking for plain truths expressed in paradox secured him a reputation for frivolity, and the fools that he did not suffer gladly were sure that the bishop did not regard serious things seriously. This was nonsense. Creighton had the brilliant teacher's instinctive gift for arresting attention, but pomposity too often saw in this only "unsoundness." It speaks well for Creighton's sweet temper and charm of manner that this reputation, which has proved fatal to many a man's career, did nothing to harm his. To his Church, Creighton stood in a simple enough relationship. His faith was commonplace; he did not fa-

[2] In the latter respect, reform is overdue.

vour the extravagances of either extreme party, and he admired
the Church quite as much for the sake of its history and institu-
tional authority as for its ministry. There was something almost
aggressively uncomplicated about Creighton.

These same gifts of straight seeing and straight thinking, down-
rightness and simplicity, mark him as an historian. Like most of
his contemporaries, he regarded Ranke as the model to imitate,
and his preoccupations were, therefore, with political history,
diplomacy, and personality. He had some small interest in social problems, the facts of the national economy, instruments of
government, but he knew little enough about them; it is quite
strange to think of him as a contemporary of Maitland and a
younger man than Stubbs. He refused to pass lofty judgments, a
restraint for which Lord Acton severely censured him; but
Creighton was right, and his notable freedom from the prejudices of his own time has allowed his work to survive, still
readable and still read. His habit of taking down the scaffold
when the building was finished and of putting a good coat of matt
paint over the whole may disguise the great learning and wide
reading that went to the making of his books. In his life of
Elizabeth, for instance, he quotes constantly from the documents
but gives not a single reference, and his quotations are not only
apposite but also correct. In short, he wrote to be read; he wrote
swift, plain, narrative history; he knew how to make events
fascinating and people alive; and he did all this with a minimum
of selfconscious art. But his equipment lacked an important professional dimension; he rarely, if ever, used manuscripts; and he
could not penetrate below the level of high politics. Curiously
enough for a cleric writing on ecclesiastical institutions and religious centuries, he did not handle at all well the facts of religion or its impact on history, and his great work on the Papacy
palpably falters when he has to turn from the politics of Renaissance Italy to the eruption of Luther.[3]

This sober, unemphatic, undogmatic attitude to religious his-

[3] Owen Chadwick, *Creighton on Luther* (inaugural lecture; Cambridge, 1959).

tory, combined with his close attachment to the kind of liberal Churchmanship which dominated the Establishment of his day, mars his account of the Elizabethan Church. That he made serious mistakes about the history of Puritanism is no blame to him; a great deal of work has been and is being done for which he lived too soon. But it is a shortcoming that he could not really understand its spirit because he disapproved of its violent enthusiasm. On the other hand, his own attitudes enabled him to do full justice to Elizabeth herself; he understood her too well to suppose, with some now current opinion, that she had no religion, and his description, in this book, of her faith is in some ways his masterpiece. The *History of the Papacy*, for sheer size alone, must remain his chief work, but yet he never did anything better than this clear delineation and sympathetic analysis of a character he thought in many ways deplorable. Unlike more recent historians of the age, he could appreciate the skills, intelligence, and achievement of the Queen without having to gloss over her evasiveness, frequent indecisiveness, bad manners, and sillinesses. "If Elizabeth had been capable of a bold policy . . . ," says Creighton outright (p. 96) on an occasion when he finds her missing her opportunities. One would look in vain for a similar condemnation—calm, measured, perhaps a trifle condescending—in the pages of Neale or A. L. Rowse. Creighton managed to admire the Queen without especially liking her or falling for her posthumous charms. In consequence, his picture of Queen Elizabeth remains in many ways the most satisfying yet painted. If it lacks some of Neale's sparkle, as well as much of the broad historical coverage he provides, it scores by a powerful strain of distance and independence in the historian. Above all, there is Creighton's very fine sense of realities. He continually persuades the reader that he knows how things happen in the realms of high policy; the master carpenter's son has a splendid way of suggesting a lifetime spent among princes and potentates. The modern mitre at first hand, the medieval tiara at second, clearly did most to shape this historian.

However, it must be said that paradoxically Creighton's success in this book owes most to his greatest failing as an historian. He did not like Elizabeth, who seemed to him a tiresome woman of somewhat shaky morals and far too little scruple, and he said at one time that he did not really like the sixteenth century at all. This comes through clearly enough in the little moralising that this uncensorious historian permitted himself. The men of Henry VIII's age were "low-minded, sensual, self-seeking, hypocritical and unscrupulous" (p. 6). No doubt many were, by the standards of a Victorian don and bishop; so were many of those that he shared his own world with. This unfortunate judg-ment, which has found wide acceptance, has often prevented a real understanding of the earlier sixteenth century. When Eliza-beth acts out a mild flirtation with a Scottish envoy (who knew how to play up to her), we are brought up standing by the com-ment: "It is impossible to say what Elizabeth meant by this con-duct" (p. 56). It is most certainly not impossible: she was amus-ing herself. And the words "this conduct," straight from the mouth of the stern moral tutor, remind us that in his young days Creighton had been a remarkable prig. Francis Bacon is censured for his cynicism which shows "that a political career was recog-nised as a form of personal adventure" (p. 180), a comment which shows that Creighton actually believed it to be something different in his own day. He should have known better. Those who in a democracy pursue power with the welfare of the peo-ple forever in their mouths have only adapted the principles of Tudor politicians who claimed to be devoted solely to the serv-ice of their prince. It is not clear whether Creighton ever really grasped the importance of royal pomp and patronage, the means by which political society was held together and managed. On the other hand, his robust view of the idiocies to which the famous love-cult of Elizabeth could descend in the hands of la-bouring courtiers is more convincing than the usual attempt to dignify them by reference to the need for queen-worship. No one denies that Gloriana found it easiest to attract loyalty by a species of elevated and formalised dalliance, but even contemporaries regarded some of the cult's manifestations with distaste, and Creighton's occasional contempt for it, modified by his understanding of its purpose, is just (for instance, pp. 175–78).

In any case, Creighton moralised very little and on the whole managed to keep the nineteenth century out of the sixteenth—much better than his friend and critic Acton. But if he did not labour his distaste for Elizabeth, he still had to overcome it, and this he achieved by a bad slip in historical understanding. What he approved was not the Queen's character, but what he persuaded himself was her true achievement. As the final pages of his book show, he believed that Elizabeth gave to England a new start in life, and that she did so because she possessed an inborn understanding of her people. Others have made much the same point, but with Creighton it ran away into a grey kind of mysticism. Elizabeth never acted "unless she felt that her people were in hearty agreement with her"; when action was called for, she did not weigh the advice of her councillors but "fell back upon her instinctive perception of what England wanted" (pp. 198–99). The "people" and a personified England crop up much too readily in this book, and what England wanted in the reign of Elizabeth was, apparently, an imperial career culminating in the late-Victorian sense of mission. Elizabeth "educated Englishmen to a perception of England's destiny" (p. 198). What destiny can she herself be shown to have been aware of? The question needs only to be asked to reveal the empty rhetoric of Creighton's assertion. In fact, Elizabeth pursued the only policy open to a sixteenth-century monarch: she promoted her country's interests by promoting her own, tried to avoid military or diplomatic defeat, tried to preserve unity at home, tried to adjust her resources to the sacred cause of public display. Certainly she sought "greatness," but if she had had to define it she would have spoken of Henry V and Henry VIII rather than of unknown lands over the seas. In so far as she was aware what English seamen were doing, it is plain that she grudgingly admitted the usefulness of piratical treasure but otherwise showed little understanding and less liking for these adventurers. They, indeed, were often moved by zeal for Queen, country, and their religion; she was not inclined to serve any of these causes in the manner of Drake and Hawkins. The people whose assent she cultivated were hardly the nation: they were that small part of her subjects, perhaps one in twelve of them, who held wealth and power in the realm and had to be kept reasonably contented as well as ruled and controlled. Creighton's unexpected lapse into cloudiness is readily explained. He was himself a fervent patriot, with a true love of his nation and its achievements. As he once said: "I am not ashamed to own that I am an Englishman first and a Churchman afterwards." [4] He lived at the height of England's greatness and showed his feelings when he followed the Unionist wing of the Liberal party in the great split of the 1880's. And so he read that greatness back to what he conceived to be its origins, implanted an absurd and anachronistic degree of foresight in Elizabeth, and spoke of the relations between Queen and people in terms more appropriate to a newspaper editorial than to a work of history.

Nevertheless, this lapse saved his book. He could, in consequence, come to study and to praise Elizabeth. Nor did he overdo the nonsense: most of the time he set her in the context of her real problems. The occasional errors corrected by later research do not matter much either, though the main ones should perhaps be briefly mentioned here. Creighton's account of the Elizabethan Church settlement of 1559 (pp. 32–33) needs to be revised in accordance with Neale's demonstration that the Queen had to make some fundamental concessions to a parliamentary lobby of extremer Protestants.[5] The theology absorbed by the English exiles during Mary's reign was Zwinglian rather than Calvinist (p. 82). Creighton was quite wrong to suppose that English wool was still being exported in quantity "a few

---

[4] It seems this remark shocked some people who, unlike Creighton, apparently supposed that Churchman equals Christian.

[5] *English Historical Review*, 1951.

years before" 1578 (p. 106); manufactured cloth had gradually replaced raw wool as England's chief export from the later fourteenth century onwards. Secretary Davison, though sacrificed in public to the Queen's anger at the execution of Mary Queen of Scots, was in fact treated very differently in private (p. 150).[6] Creighton's account of the Armada campaign is marred by traditional error; the story has now been told fully and brilliantly by Garrett Mattingly.[7] On Puritanism and Parliament, Creighton's few words need to be vastly supplemented by much recent work.[8]

More important than the obvious detailed deficiencies of an older book are the points of interpretation on which it is not easy to agree with Creighton's views. That Elizabeth's definition of the royal supremacy over the Church "reserved the freedom of the Church" in any way, that she deliberately avoided interference in its affairs (p. 34–35), is hard to credit when one remembers her use of ecclesiastical commissions, her suspension of Archbishop Grindal, and her personal activity against parliamentary intervention in matters spiritual. Creighton may have meant that the Queen was no pope—that she did not personally define doctrine or administer the Church—which is true; but what he actually said cannot be maintained. The Elizabethan Church was inexorably under the control of its supreme governor. The explanation, offered on p. 155, for Elizabeth's inability to act decisively grows out of Creighton's mystical concepts; there is absolutely no evidence that the Queen held that the country would "grow into a new consciousness of its position if it had time for reflection and experiment," no probability that anyone thought along such lines or would have been

[6] R. B. Wernham, in *English Historical Review*, 1931.

[7] *The Defeat of the Spanish Armada* (New York and London, 1959).

[8] Especially J. E. Neale, *Elizabeth I and her Parliaments* (2 vols.; London, 1953 and 1957). See in general for work done in Elizabethan history since Creighton's day, Conyers Read, *Bibliography of British History: the Tudor Period* (2nd ed., Oxford, 1959), and a shorter but more recent list in G. R. Elton, *England under the Tudors* (London, ed. of 1962).

well advised to do so, nor the slightest sign that the Queen was even capable of that kind of thought. The whole of those two pages is sheer conjecture, and very unconvincing conjecture at that. As a rule, Elizabeth avoided action because the dilemmas were too formidable, because she was temperamentally inclined to procrastination, and because she had found by experience that her problems were often better solved by being left undecided for a while. Creighton's Elizabeth is at this point a highly unlikely mixture of minor prophet and mother hen. It may also be doubted whether the aftermath of the Armada campaign produced the confidence and release from fear which Creighton thought he saw (p. 156). He was seemingly not aware that the war never went so well again as at its beginning; and the 1590's, troubled by plague, bad harvests, and heavy taxation, were years of unrest and unease rather than this fine confident morning of Creighton's imagining. For myself, I also cannot accept his explanation of Elizabeth's very unpleasant and often hysterical reaction to marriage among her courtiers and entourage (p. 161). The truth is that she resented others marrying when she herself had not been able to follow her inclination by doing so, though it must be added that secret marriages, especially among people close to the Tudor family, were in the unsettled state of the succession a real political problem. But who had left it unsettled?

These are all, however, points of no overwhelming significance. One would hope that after seventy years of energetic historical research and writing a book's details would require revision, and that even its main interpretative approach might seem improbable. Creighton's life of Elizabeth comes remarkably well out of so searching a test. That is not to say that a new study of the Queen is not highly desirable. It is now over thirty years since Neale's book appeared, and these thirty years have added a large amount of knowledge and understanding, much of it owing to Neale himself. There are things about both Creighton's and Neale's Elizabeth that it is no longer easy to accept. The first has been sufficiently criticised here; as to the second, it might be said that that paragon of unfailing political skill arouses suspicion when time and again she is found in crises both internal and external into which she can be seen to have slipped either by her refusal to make up her mind or by her arrogant assertion of her prerogative. It looks, in fact, as though the next biographer of Elizabeth would do well to test Neale's Queen by the criteria and with the detachment used by Creighton. One can only hope that he will write as well as those two predecessors and contribute as lasting a work to English historical literature.

G. R. ELTON

Clare College
University of Cambridge

Preface to the 1899 Edition

⌒§ The object which I had before me in writing the following pages was to sketch the life of Elizabeth as plainly as possible. I have endeavoured to illustrate a character rather than to write the history of a time. But Elizabeth's life was so closely interwoven with the history of England that it is impossible to separate her actions from public affairs, and I have been drawn into general history more often than I wished. I can only say that I have endeavoured not to wander into any matters which were not necessary for an explanation of Elizabeth's conduct, and that I have only enlarged the stage to find room for the actor.

It was impossible within my limits to do more than sketch a rough outline of a very complex personality, which reflected only too faithfully the perplexities of a very difficult time. Such an attempt was only possible owing to the amount of detailed work which has already been done by others. But it seemed to me that the outline must be clearly drawn before the amazing varieties of expression could be understood. Bewildering as they were in any particular matter, they all had reference to certain central conceptions. It is these which I tried to discover and exhibit.

M. LONDON.

February, 1899.

Contents

CONTENTS

Queen Elizabeth

I

THE YOUTH OF
ELIZABETH

⋄⋄ The Princess Elizabeth of England was born at Greenwich, between three and four of the afternoon of September 7, 1533. Her birth was a matter of small rejoicing to her parents, who were sorely disappointed that their first-born was not a boy. Seldom had greater issues depended on the sex of a child than were now at stake. Henry VIII. pined for a male heir to succeed to the English throne. He had wearied of his Spanish wife, Catherine; he had made the hand of his sole daughter, Mary, the bait of many an alliance, which had come to nought. He had wasted England's resources on foreign wars, which had brought no return. He had found Catherine, with her devotion to Spain and her nephew, Charles V., an obstacle to his political plans, and had wearied of her person. He had lost his heart to Anne Boleyn, and determined to make her Queen at all costs. For this purpose he had waded deeply in the mire, had broken through all the conventions of propriety, had quarrelled with Pope and Emperor, and had filled Europe with his clamorous assertions of the right of a King of England to have his own way in matters matrimonial. When he failed of immediate success, he had set on foot a revolutionary change in England itself, the end of which he could not foresee. He had stubbornly declared his intention to be divorced from Catherine and to marry Anne; he was bent on discovering some means of effecting his object.

The death of Archbishop Warham in August, 1532, opened up a way. Warham had refused to consider the question of granting a divorce in England; but Henry might secure a successor to

Warham who would be amenable to his wishes. So sure was
Henry of this result that on September 1 he created Anne Marchioness of Pembroke, and presented her with jewels taken from
the Queen. This was regarded as an announcement that Anne had
consented to become the King's mistress, which was probably the
fact. Pope Clement VII. thought that such an arrangement would
end the question of the King's divorce, and accepted the royal
nomination of Thomas Cranmer as Archbishop of Canterbury in
Warham's stead. But before the bulls for his confirmation had arrived, Anne was with child, and it was necessary for her offspring
to be born in lawful wedlock. She was privately married to
Henry sometime in January, 1533. Cranmer was consecrated
Archbishop on March 30. On May 10, he opened his court to inquire into the validity of the King's marriage with Catherine. Before the end of the month he pronounced the marriage with
Catherine to have been null and void from the beginning, and the
marriage with Anne to be good and valid. On June 1, Anne was
crowned in Westminster.

These were not creditable proceedings to submit to the judgment of the English people. They were not attached to Catherine, and they ardently wished for a male successor to the throne.
They had not sympathised with the King's foreign policy, and
they longed to be free from its complications, and manage their
national concerns in peace. They had no love for the Pope, and
wished priests and monks to be reduced to their due place in the
new society which was slowly coming into existence. They were
desirous of more common-sense and simplicity in religious matters, and had little sympathy with the old-fashioned pretentious-
ness of the Churchmen. They were quite willing that the King
should manage his personal matters as he thought best, provided
he left them in peace. But still, when all had been done and settled, they shook their heads, and felt that there had been at work
an amount of trickery and injustice which they could not approve. They were not critics of the King's proceedings, and they
were ready to wait; but their sympathy was more with the de-

graded Queen than with her upstart and brazen successor. The birth of a male heir to the throne would have gone far to reconcile them with what had been done. It would have satisfied the general desire that there should be no difficulties about the succession, that England should not have to face domestic discord and foreign intrigue. But another girl was a hindrance rather than a help to future prospects. If the choice was to lie between her and Mary, the claims of Mary would stand higher.

So the birth of Elizabeth was a disappointment to her parents, and was the beginning of a cooling of Henry's affections towards the wife whom he had braved so much to gain. There was not much heartiness in the rejoicings which announced her coming into the world, or in the magnificence which attended her baptism on September 10, when her godparents were Archbishop Cranmer, the Dowager-Duchess of Norfolk, and the Dowager-Marchioness of Dorset. Three months after this a separate establishment was assigned to the child at Hatfield, where she was joined by her unfortunate sister Mary. The child saw little of her mother. Once only do we find her mentioned at Court. It was on January 9, 1536 when the news of the death of Queen Catherine had just arrived. Henry appeared dressed all in yellow, save for a white plume in his cap. After dinner he carried Elizabeth in his arms round the room, and showed her with triumph to the assembled courtiers. Anne joined in Henry's triumph, but her joy was of short duration. Henry was weary of Anne, and her failure to bear other children made her useless. So long as Catherine lived he was bound to endure her vanity, her bad temper, and her want of tact and personal dignity. After Catherine's death he resolved to rid himself of her; and Cromwell thought it better to ruin her entirely rather than divorce her on some technical plea. Anne was accused of repeated acts of adultery and incest, throughout all the period of her married life. She was found guilty and was executed on May 19, 1536. Two days before her death her marriage was declared invalid from the beginning, and Elizabeth was thus pronounced to be illegitimate.

This was a tragic beginning of the life of one of the greatest of the rulers of England, and it is tempting to consider the influence of heredity on Elizabeth's character. In her great qualities of caution and prudence she reverted to her grandfather, Henry VII., while from her father she inherited the royal imperiousness and personal charm which always secured his popularity. To her mother she owed her vanity, her unscrupulousness, her relentless and overbearing temper. Anne Boleyn has been hardly judged. Indeed her position was impossible from the beginning; and none but a coarse, ambitious and self-seeking woman would have struggled so desperately as she did for a prize which was sure to be fatal. Her hardness and coarseness passed to her daughter, in whom they were modified by finer qualities, and were curbed by a sense of duty. But Elizabeth always remained more truly the daughter of Anne Boleyn than of Henry VIII., though she never took any steps to clear the character of her mother, whom indeed she was anxious to forget.

The day after Anne's execution Henry married Jane Seymour, and Elizabeth was banished from her father's sight. She was committed to the care of Lady Bryan, a relative of her mother, and was assigned as a residence, Hunsdon House, in Hertfordshire, pleasantly situated on a hill overlooking the Stort river. With her was her half-sister Mary, now twenty years of age, devoted to the memory of her mother, and vainly endeavouring to soften the inhumanity of the King.

At first, Elizabeth was entirely neglected by her father. Lady Bryan was driven to write to Cromwell that the child was almost without clothes; she begged that provision should be made for her needs. Her remonstrance seems to have had some effect; and she did her best to discharge her duty to the child intrusted to her care. Elizabeth was well brought up. She was taught to behave with decorum. She learnt to sew, and at the age of six presented her brother Edward with a shirt of cambric of her own working. Edward was also committed to the charge of Lady Bryan, and for some time the two children were educated together. They were willing pupils, for the Tudors were fond of learning. They rose early and devoted the first part of the day to religious instruction. Then they studied "languages, or some of the liberal sciences, or moral learning collected out of such authors as did best conduce to the instruction of Princes". When Edward went to exercise in the open air, Elizabeth, "in her private chamber, betook herself to her lute or viol, and, wearied with that, to practise her needle".

Their teachers were carefully chosen from the best scholars of the time. First came Richard Cox, who had been trained in Wolsey's new College at Oxford, and whom Elizabeth afterwards made Bishop of Ely, in remembrance of her Latin lessons. After Cox came the great Cambridge scholar, Sir John Cheke, who carried on their education in the Classics. With him was Roger Ascham, who did not disdain to teach them writing, and formed that bold handwriting which characterises them both, and was a product of a time when writing was still considered as a fine art. Besides them were learned masters in French and Italian. Elizabeth showed such proficiency in these languages that, at the age of eleven, she wrote an Italian letter to Queen Catherine Parr, and also sent a translation of a book of devotions, *Le Miroir de l'Ame pécheresse*, written by Margaret of Valois, sister of Francis I.

While she was thus carefully educated in mind and body, Elizabeth had no education of her affections. Her father seldom saw her and took no interest in her. She was separated from her brother Edward, and was settled by herself at Enfield. As soon as she could think for herself, she must have felt that she was surrounded by an atmosphere of suspicion, and was alone and friendless in the world. The death of Henry, in 1547, did not remove this isolation. The young Edward was separated from his sisters; and they were carefully kept apart. In fact, the accession of Edward VI. opened the way for deep laid political intrigues. The boy was sickly, and was not likely to come to years of discretion. It is true that Henry VIII. had, by his will, made tardy reparation to the daughters whom he had so deeply wronged, and recognised their right of succession. But Henry's will was not of much value. The Council which he had provided was set aside by the influence of Edward's uncle, Edward Seymour, who took the rank of Duke of Somerset and the title of Lord Protector. Others, however, were not likely to acquiesce in his supremacy; and Mary and Elizabeth might be instruments in their hands.

Elizabeth was committed to the care of the Queen-Dowager, Catherine Parr; but she had a house of her own and a retinue of a hundred and twenty attendants. Her governess was a relative by her mother's side, Catherine Ashley, a foolish and imprudent woman, little capable of guiding the precocious girl amid the dangers which beset her. Elizabeth was soon to learn the lessons of life in a way which indelibly impressed them upon her mind. We may pity a girl exposed to such temptations; but we must admit that there was little intuitive modesty in a character which could not resist their grossness.

The matrimonial proceedings of Henry VIII. had necessarily lowered the tone of morality amongst his courtiers. The coarse gossip which was prevalent was degrading and removed all sense of restraint. The great social revolution through which England was passing gave scope to unlimited covetousness. Men were low-minded, sensual, self-seeking, hypocritical and unscrupulous. There was a feeling that they were sharing in a general scramble, and that he was cleverest who gained most. There was little sense of honour, or of family affection. The fact that Somerset had won the first place was resented by his brother Thomas, Lord Seymour of Sudeley, who was made Lord High Admiral. His first plan was to marry Elizabeth; but this required the consent of the King and Council, and he knew that their consent would not be given. He then approached the Queen-Dowager, whose lover he had been before her marriage with Henry VIII., and secretly married her within a few months after Henry's death. The marriage was reluctantly sanctioned in June, 1547. Lord Seymour was now brought nearer to the young King, and had the guardianship of Elizabeth. He was a tall, handsome man; and Catherine was devoted to him. At first, she thought no harm of the familiarity with which he began to treat the young girl who was now thrown in his way. But it soon became evident, even to her, that Seymour was making love to Elizabeth in a corrupting way, and that Elizabeth showed no displeasure at his revolting attentions. Catherine Ashley was an accomplice, discussed with Elizabeth the attentions of her admirer, and connived at water-parties by night on the Thames. Things went so far that, at last, the Queen-Dowager could endure Elizabeth's presence no longer, but dismissed her from her house in May, 1548. This was done without any open scandal; the cause was kept a profound secret. Elizabeth was established at Cheshunt, and friendly correspondence continued between her and her former friends. Everything was done to repair past indiscretion and let it sink into oblivion.

Catherine, however, was deeply wounded and could not forget. On August 30 she bore a daughter, and died a week afterwards. On her deathbed, she said sadly: "Those that be about me care not for me, but stand laughing at my grief; and the more good I will to them the less good they will to me". Seymour answered: "Why, sweetheart, I could you no hurt". The dying woman said aloud: "No, my Lord, I think so;" then she added in a whisper "but, my Lord, you have given me many shrewd taunts".

Seymour, however, felt no remorse for his treatment of a wife who bequeathed him all that she possessed. Scarcely was she buried before he resumed his intrigues for gaining power by a new combination. He had bought from her father the wardship of the Lady Jane Grey, whom he kept in his house and designed to marry to the young King, while he himself married Elizabeth. He opened communications through Catherine Ashley, who told Elizabeth that Seymour, who would fain have married her before he married the Queen, would soon come to woo. Elizabeth was certainly pleased at the prospect, and encouraged the proposal. But Seymour, ambitious as he was, could not conceal his projects, and Somerset was resolved to rid himself of his audacious brother. In January, 1549, Lord Seymour was arrested on a charge of high treason. Elizabeth's governess, Catherine Ashley, and her steward, Thomas Parry, were carried away and imprisoned in the Tower. Elizabeth herself was confined to her house at Hatfield, under the guardianship of Sir Robert Tyrwhit, who was charged by the Council to examine her and discover evidence against Seymour.

It was a terrible position for a young girl who was not yet sixteen. Deprived of her only friends, not knowing what they might reveal, left alone to the mercy of an astute official, whose duty it was to examine her from day to day, and make her admit her guilt, she well might quail. Her honour, even her life, was at stake. She was at the mercy of her servants. She had not the unconsciousness of absolute innocence; and could only confide in the fidelity of her imprisoned attendants and in her own dexterity. At first, she burst into a flood of tears, and Tyrwhit thought that his task would be easy. He advised her to confess everything; the evil and shame would be ascribed to Catherine Ashley; she would be forgiven on the score of her youth. But Elizabeth soon regained her self-command in the face of danger. He could get nothing from her: "and yet," he writes, "I can see from her face that she is guilty, but she will abide more storms before she accuse Mrs. Ashley". The next day he succeeded no better, and could only repeat, "I do assure your Grace she hath a very good wit, and nothing is gotten of her but by great policy". Elizabeth would not commit herself, and in a week's time felt sufficiently secure of the reticence of her servants to write in a dignified strain to the Protector, defending her reputation and protecting her innocence. "My conscience," she wrote, "beareth me witness, which I would not for all earthly things offend in anything, for I know I have a soul to save, as well as other folks have, wherefore I will above all things have respect unto this same."

As nothing could be discovered from Elizabeth, Tyrwhit turned his attention to her imprisoned steward, Parry, and extracted from him an account of the unseemly familiarities between his mistress and Lord Seymour. Catherine Ashley could not deny her knowledge of them, and furnished a few more particulars. Then Tyrwhit returned to Elizabeth and put the two confessions into her hand. She read them abashed and breathless. But when Tyrwhit told her that Catherine Ashley would say nothing till she was confronted with Parry, the Tudor rage broke forth. "False wretch," she cried, "he promised not to confess to death; how could he make such a promise and break it?" Yet, downcast as she was at reading the record of her indiscretion, she soon recovered her presence of mind. She saw that on the main points her servants had stood firm. They sacrificed Elizabeth's private character to maintain her political innocence. She had been a shameless flirt, but had never contemplated marrying Seymour without the consent of the Council. Elizabeth took her cue accordingly. Tyrwhit could extract nothing from her except scraps of foolish conversation about the possibility of such a marriage, in answer to which suggestions she always reserved the Council's assent. "They all sing the same song," said Tyrwhit wearily, "and so I think they would not do unless they had got the note before." After all his efforts, the girl of sixteen baffled the experienced man of affairs.

The Council proceeded against Seymour on other grounds, but administered a rebuke to Elizabeth in a letter which informed her: "Catherine Ashley, who hithertofore hath had the special charge to see to the good education and government of your person, hath shown herself far unmeet to occupy any such place longer about your Grace. Being informed that she hath not shewed herself so much attendant to her office in this past as we looked for at her hands, we have thought good somewhat to say roundly to her in that behalf." Elizabeth was informed that Lady Tyrwhit had been appointed in Catherine Ashley's stead, and was recommended to follow her good advice. At first, Elizabeth was furious. She would have no mistress save Catherine Ashley; she had not behaved so as to deserve the change. She wept all night,

and sulked all the following day. Her mood was changed by a letter from the Protector, which told her that Seymour's household
was broken up, and enabled her to see that his ruin was imminent.
Then Elizabeth's spirit began to droop, though she vigorously defended Seymour if anything was said against him. She wrote to
the Protector, remonstrating at the removal of Catherine Ashley
as likely to corroborate the rumours which were current about
her conduct. She asked that these rumours might be contradicted
by a proclamation. This last request was gratified. But one of the
articles against Seymour was that he had "attempted and gone
about to marry the King's Majesty's sister, the Lady Elizabeth,
second inheritor in remainder to the Crown". On March 20,
1549, Seymour's head fell on the scaffold.

This was a crushing experience for a girl of sixteen. It was undoubtedly the great crisis of Elizabeth's life, and did more than
anything else to form her character. She learned, and she never
forgot the lesson, that it was dangerous to follow her inclinations
and indulge her affections. She dearly loved Seymour, with the
ardour of a passionate girl. She was on the brink of a secret marriage with him, though she knew his coarse character and had
been witness of the unhappiness of his former wife. She had a
strong feeling of attachment for Catherine Ashley, and had
trusted to her discretion. She learned the limitations of human
trustworthiness, the inevitableness of personal responsibility. All
this was an unwelcome revelation of life and its issues to herself.
She must trust in herself and in herself only. Rigorous self-
repression and self-restraint could alone enable her to stand securely. Love, trust, confidence were all beset with dangers. In the
quietness which followed this period of trial she thought out the
meaning of what she had endured. She had loved, and her lover
had perished. She could ask herself what that love had meant to
her. Was it more than a temporary stirring of the senses? Was it
worth the risk which she had run, the imprudence which she had
committed? What would have been her future had she married
Seymour? Was he capable of loving her in return, or was she

merely a puppet in his hands, a piece in his game of political self-seeking? She must have recalled his treatment of the Queen-Dowager, whose tears she had seen flow, whose dying words of disappointment had been repeated to her. At the time, secure in her own youthful charms, she had thought disdainfully of the middle-aged queen. If she had become Seymour's wife, would she have been any the happier? Would not she too have been abandoned when her usefulness was past? She had seen the Lady Jane Grey, an inmate of Seymour's house, another girl whose hand was of value for an intriguer to dispose of. What place had love in such matters as these? It was possible for a village maiden: it was an impossible luxury for one who had a shred of claim to the throne of England.

We know how thoroughly Elizabeth understood these truths and acted upon them later. Her success in so doing was due to the severe teaching of experience. When she recovered from the shock of Seymour's death and could look around her, she saw that it was necessary to recover her character and restore her reputation. No one could be better fitted to help her than Lady Tyrwhit, who was a wise, sympathetic and pious woman. She had formed one of the household of the Queen-Dowager, knew what Elizabeth had gone through, and could talk to her freely about the past. Under her care Elizabeth once more lived a quiet and studious life, principally at Hatfield. Ascham was summoned to be her tutor and was astonished at the rapidity of her progress. When she had just entered her seventeenth year she could speak French and Italian as well as English; Latin with ease, Greek moderately. But her taste for literature was genuine: she appreciated nice distinctions in the use of words, and was a severe critic of style. She read with Ascham nearly the whole of Cicero and Livy, Sophocles, and several orations of Isocrates, besides the Greek Testament, the writings of St. Cyprian and the Commonplaces of Melanchthon. She was fond of music, but did not devote much time to it, nor to dress, in which she loved simplicity.

Her literary tastes were enduring; her love of simplicity soon passed away. Indeed, it was never real, and Ascham's mention of it shows that Elizabeth was acting a part. She had been detected as a shameless coquette; she adopted the attitude of a modest and pious maiden. It was the wisest thing which she could do; for the times were stormy, and their signs were hard to read. Before the end of 1550 the Protector's power had fallen before the superior craft of John Dudley, Earl of Warwick. Warwick's plans were deeper than those of Somerset, and required greater preparation. As the first step towards a distinctive policy, Warwick allied himself with the more advanced reformers in religion, and demanded strict uniformity of religious practise. This entirely accorded with the views of the young King. But there was one who could not be induced to swerve from her former habit, the Princess Mary; and all efforts to subdue her obstinacy were in vain. It was at this time that Elizabeth was summoned to Court (March, 1551) to act as a foil to the recalcitrant Mary. Elizabeth appeared with studious simplicity and Edward welcomed her as "his dear and sweet sister, Temperance". Elizabeth had achieved her end. She had established her character. Her "maidenly apparel," we are told, "made the noblemen's wives and daughters ashamed to be dressed and painted like peacocks". She was in a fair way to become the idol of the reforming party.

She returned to Hatfield well satisfied with her position, which she maintained with quiet splendour. Her household accounts for the year from October, 1551, to October, 1552, have been preserved and give us an insight into her daily life. Her income was nearly £6000 a year, equivalent to £30,000 of our money. Her expenditure was mostly spent in maintaining her establishment and dispensing hospitality. Her kitchen account was £500, besides £312 for poultry; her bakehouse cost £212; wax candles and spices amounted to £340; wages to £426; and wine and beer to £306. She spent little on her dress, less on her books; and her alms only reached the moderate sum of £7 17s. She made some profit by selling things to the royal household. The accounts themselves were submitted to her and she signed as auditor at the bottom of several pages. It is clear that she was a prudent and thrifty manager, and at the end of the year had a balance in her favour of £1500. She early developed that financial carefulness which was not the smallest element in her subsequent success.

New perils, however, were gathering round her. Edward VI. was visibly dying; and the schemes of Warwick, who had been created Duke of Northumberland, began to take shape. He worked, upon the King's earnest desire, for the establishment of Protestantism in England and for its future maintenance. To this primary object all else must give way. If Henry VIII. could dispose of the succession by his will, so could his son. It was not fitting that Henry's daughters should succeed their brother. Mary was a favourer of the old religion. She could be set aside on the ground of illegitimacy, and the same plea must include Elizabeth also. The line of Henry's elder sister, Margaret of Scotland, was to be passed over for that of the younger sister Mary, and the crown conferred on the Lady Jane Grey, who was married to a son of Northumberland. To clear the ground for this arrangement a marriage had been proposed between Elizabeth and the King of Denmark. The proposal came to nothing. When Edward VI. died, July 6, 1553, all was ready for the proclamation of the Lady Jane, and the imprisonment and death of Mary and Elizabeth.

Mary was the more important, and must be secured at once. Northumberland hid the fact of the King's death, and invited Mary to her brother's deathbed. But Mary was informed of the truth, while on her way, and took refuge in Norfolk. It was necessary for Northumberland to go in pursuit of her, a comparatively easy matter. But Northumberland had not counted on Mary's resoluteness, and on the objection of the English people to revolutions. Mary summoned the people to her side as their lawful Queen, and they answered her call. The victory of Northumberland, they saw, would mean a long period of disquiet, and insecurity of life and property. Town after town declared in

Mary's favour, and before Northumberland could reach her she was guarded by an army of 40,000 men. The scheme to dispossess her completely failed.

Elizabeth, meanwhile, remained quietly at Hatfield, whence she wrote to congratulate Mary on her accession. She came to London to greet the Queen on her entrance, August 3, 1553. Mary received her graciously and gave her the chief place after herself, though she must have known that the graceful figure and youthful vivacity of Elizabeth threw into the shade her own careworn face, grown old before its time. Doubtless, Mary wished to do her duty by her sister; but each must have felt that there was a gulf of separation between the daughter of Catherine and the daughter of Anne Boleyn. The one passionately desired to wipe away all that happened since the days when Catherine stood by the side of Henry, his undoubted wife. The other must have marvelled sometimes at the thoughts of all that had occurred to call her into being; she must have felt that she embodied in herself the principles of a mighty revolution. This difference between the two sisters was inevitable. It showed itself at once, when Mary did not attend the funeral of Edward, but was present at a Requiem Mass in the chapel of the Tower. She invited Elizabeth to accompany her, but Elizabeth declined. Mary would not brook resistance to her will. Either Elizabeth must conform to her religious practises, or else must leave the Court.

Elizabeth's position was difficult. She had been brought up in the religious ideas which prevailed in directing the policy of Henry VIII., the acceptance of the results of the New Learning, and the reform of the Church in accordance with a fuller understanding of the Scriptures and of Christian antiquity. She had no sympathy with the more advanced views of Continental Protestantism, which had been favoured by Northumberland for the purpose of forming a party in England which depended on himself. That party had fallen, and Mary was bent upon using her victory to restore the old Church. How far that was possible remained to be seen. This, at all events, was certain, that the

Church could never again be what it had been in the days of Wolsey. Its exact form remained to be determined. Mary's personal opinions could not be impressed upon the English people all at once. For this reason she was anxious that they should be adopted by those immediately around her; and, first of all, by Elizabeth. Elizabeth felt that, if she was entirely obstinate, she would seem to identify herself with the Protestant party, which, though fallen for a time, was sure to raise its head. If she did so, she would expose herself to suspicion, and would be regarded as a source of political danger to Mary. She knew that already the foreign ambassadors advised Mary to remove from her path one who was her natural rival. Whatever else might happen, Elizabeth had no wish to appear as the champion of the party of Northumberland. Accordingly she determined to maintain her own religious position as nearly as she could in the circumstances. To refuse obstinately to go to Mass would be to declare herself a Protestant in the political sense. To go to Mass without a protest would be to declare herself an adherent of the Pope. To go to Mass with marked unwillingness, in obedience to the Queen's wishes, was to declare herself of the same mind as the great majority of the English people, resolute in her adhesion to the principles of what had been done in reforming the English Church, but uncertain under what forms this could best be maintained. She professed herself ready to surrender her own prejudices and went to Mass with the Queen on September 8, with a downcast look, complaining of illness on the way. After this concession on her part she was given the first place after the Queen at the ceremony of the Coronation on October I. Elizabeth knew the value of this public recognition, and felt that for the present she had done all that could be done. She saw that, amid the intrigues which gathered round Mary, her own position in the court was dangerous. She had the wisdom to withdraw in time. After several requests, she obtained permission to depart and set out for her house of Ashridge, on December 6. No sooner had she arrived than she wrote to Mary for ornaments for her chapel. She knew Mary's weak side. She chose to represent herself as one who was seeking her way back to the true Church.

Few women have been more unhappy than Mary Tudor. She came to the throne with a mind embittered by the sense of past wrongs, with no friend whom she could trust, and no coun-sellor strong enough to advise her. She was strangely isolated from the actual politics of England. How was she to be attached to them? Her advisers were agreed that she must marry, and doubtless hoped to manage the Queen through her husband. There was a candidate ready to hand, Edward Courtenay, Earl of Devon, who had been imprisoned in the Tower for the last four-teen years through Henry VIII.'s jealousy of any pretender to the Crown. Courtenay's grandmother was a daughter of Edward IV., and he represented the White Rose. For this cause his father had been beheaded; his mother and himself, a boy of twelve, confined within the Tower, whence Mary had released him. His birth, his sad story, his handsome face, and his accomplishments made him popular; and there was a general desire that he should marry the Queen. Had Courtenay been a wiser man, the course of affairs might have been different. But, on his release, he plunged into every kind of folly and excess. Mary had no liking for such a husband. Her eyes were already turned elsewhere. She was de-voted to her cousin, the Emperor Charles V., who had always ap-peared to her as the chivalrous defender of her luckless mother. In the long hours of her solitude she had nourished a fantastic reverence for him. She longed to be allied to her mother's house. On his side, Charles V. cherished a dream of universal monarchy, towards which a close hold on England would greatly help. So Charles, through his ambassadors in England, became the director of Mary's policy and cautiously prepared the way for her mar-riage with his son Philip. But no caution could overcome the re-pugnance of the English people to this invitation of a foreigner to mix in English affairs. It was in vain to represent to Mary the dangers which she ran. "Rather death," she said, "than marriage with any one save the Prince of Spain."

English patriotism was severely shocked at this prospect, and all who had any motive for disliking Mary's policy combined against her. Behind the English rebels stood France, which was alarmed at the accession of power to its rival, Spain. Early in 1554, a rebellion against Mary broke out in various parts of England. It was easily put down in Devonshire and in the Midlands, but in Kent Sir Thomas Wyatt repulsed the Royal forces and advanced against London. Mary was lost if she did not assure the fidelity of the citizens. But Mary had no doubt of the justice of her cause and showed no fear. She summoned the citizens to the Guildhall and there addressed them in her deep man's voice, with dignified eloquence. The city was won for the throne. Wyatt's attack failed, and he was made prisoner on February 7.

It was obvious that this insurrection was in favour of Elizabeth. Her name and Courtenay's had been on the lips of the rebels. A copy of a letter from her to the Queen was found in an intercepted dispatch of the French ambassador; Wyatt had sent her a message to withdraw from Ashridge to Dunnington. Elizabeth's conduct was that of one who waited to see the issue. Mary wrote to her on January 26, expressing fears for her safety and summoning her to London. Elizabeth answered that she was too ill to travel, and asked her to send one of her own physicians. She kept to her bed and fortified her house at Ashridge against a surprise.

On receiving this answer, Mary was too busy in defending herself to think much of her sister; but when the danger was over, the imperial ambassador pressed for vengeance. It was his interest to remove every one who might be an obstacle in the way of the Emperor's plan of attaching England to the Spanish monarchy. So long as Elizabeth lived she was a source of danger, and this was a good opportunity for silencing her for ever. Mary, however, was averse to bloodshed. The luckless Lady Jane Grey paid the penalty of her unworthy father's treason; but Elizabeth could not safely be condemned unless there was clear evidence against her. Mary showed her intention to proceed with strict regard for justice by sending an escort to bring Elizabeth to London, and placing at its head her great uncle, Lord William Howard.

Howard was aware of the importance of gaining time, and due regard was paid to Elizabeth's illness. Leaving Ashridge on February 12, she travelled only six or seven miles a day, and did not reach Highgate till the 15th. There she lay ill of the dropsy, her limbs so swollen that she could go no further. She did not enter London till the 22nd; seated in an open litter, dressed in white, with pale and haughty face, she was carried to Whitehall amid the respectful silence of the crowd.

The rebel leaders confessed that their plan had been to place Elizabeth and Courtenay on the throne. Courtenay knew of their intention; it was not certain that Elizabeth did. Strong as were the suspicions against her, nothing could be definitely proved. Moreover, the Council was divided in opinion. Many members, chief amongst whom was Gardiner, were still opposed to the Spanish marriage, and would not do anything that could help it on. Still, Elizabeth's enemies so far prevailed that on March 19 she was committed to the Tower. When this order was brought to Elizabeth she asked permission to write to the Queen. This was given, and sitting down, she wrote a letter of rugged eloquence and force. She protested her innocence, and begged for a personal interview before she was condemned to imprisonment. "You shall never by report know," she continued, "unless by yourself you hear. I have heard in my time of many cast away for want of coming to the presence of the Prince. And in late days, I heard my Lord of Somerset say, that if his brother had been suffered to speak with him, he had never suffered. But the persuasions were made to him so great that he was brought to believe that he could not live safely if the Admiral lived; and that made him consent to his death. Though these persons are not to be compared to your Majesty, yet I pray God that evil persuasions persuade not one sister against the other; and all for that they have heard false report and not hearken to the truth knowing. Therefore once again, kneeling with humbleness of heart, because I am not suffered to bow the knees of my body, I humbly crave to speak with your Highness: which I could not be so bold to desire if I knew not myself most clear as I know myself most true. And, as for the traitor Wyatt, he might peradventure write me a letter; but, on my faith, I never received any from him. And as for the copy of my letter sent to the French King, I pray God confound me eternally, if ever I sent him word, message, token or letter by any means. And to this truth, I will stand to the death."

No answer was sent to this letter, and Mary rebuked her officers for not punctually doing their duty. Next day, it was Palm Sunday, Elizabeth was taken in a barge to the Tower. At first she refused to alight at the Traitor's Gate, saying she was no traitor. "There is no choice," said one of the Lords, at the same time offering her his cloak as a protection from the rain. She "put it back with a good dash," and setting her foot down the stair, said: "Here landeth as true a subject, being prisoner, as ever landed at these stairs, and before Thee, O God, I speak it, having none other friend but Thee alone". There was no doubt about Elizabeth's courage and presence of mind. Her letter was written in her usual handwriting, and shows no sign of haste. Its characters are bold; no flourish is omitted in the signature. Not only was Elizabeth brave, but she was careful to show her bravery.

For two months she remained a close prisoner in the Tower, while her fate was a matter of daily debate. Wyatt was executed, without having said anything which incriminated her. At last, through weariness, it was agreed that her life should be spared. But she was undoubtedly dangerous, as a centre of intrigues; and it was impossible to think that she would not give them encouragement. It would be unwise to release her to live in her own house; so the royal manor of Woodstock was chosen as a place where she could be closely guarded. She was committed to the charge of Sir Henry Bedingfield, whose father had been the guardian of Queen Catherine during her imprisonment at Kimbolton. She left London on May 19, and in five days reached

Woodstock, where she had scanty accommodation assigned her in the gatehouse. Bedingfield was provided with strict orders by the Council and was over-weighted by the sense of his responsibility. After her accession, Elizabeth said to him: "If we have any prisoner whom we would have sharply and straitly kept, we will send for you". Yet she bore him no ill-will, and recognised that he only obeyed orders. Indeed she must have felt that she was a troublesome captive and often tried him to the utmost.

At first, she had neither books, nor pen and ink. When one of her attendants sent her a copy of Cicero's *De Officiis* and the Psalms in Latin, he was reproved by Bedingfield, who felt it his duty to consult the Council before permitting the use of books. When leave was given, Elizabeth asked for an English Bible, which seemed to savour heresy, as she could read Latin equally well. This new question was referred to the Council, and Elizabeth slipped in a request that she might be permitted to write to the Queen. This was granted, and Elizabeth wrote a fervent protestation of her innocence. Mary answered to Bedingfield that she had no confidence in her protestations, and ended, "wherefore our pleasure is not to be hereafter any more molested with such disguise and colourable letters". Mary, at least, had made up her mind about Elizabeth's character, and Bedingfield found some difficulty in reducing his message to terms of decent courtesy.

Elizabeth was left to her solitary reflections, ill-supplied with books or occupation, restricted in her walks in Woodstock Park, and always under the eye of Bedingfield, who reported to the Council her outbursts of temper as she chafed under this intolerable restraint. She envied the milk-maids, whose song she heard in the distance, and longed to exchange her life for theirs. She wrote in charcoal on a shutter the following lines expressing her feelings of despair:—

> *Oh Fortune, how thy restless wavering state*
> *Hath wrought with cares my troubled wit,*
> *Witness this present prison, whither fate*

Could bear me, and the joys I quit.
Thou caus'dst the guilty to be loosed
From bands wherein are innocents enclosed,
Causing the guiltless to be strait reserved
And freeing those that death had well deserved
But by her envy can be nothing wrought:
So God send to my foes all they have wrought.
Quoth Elizabeth, Prisoner

Elizabeth owed her deliverance from captivity to the influence of Philip. When Mary's marriage had been accomplished, and the supremacy of the Pope had been restored, above all, when Mary was supposed to be with child, there was no longer the same need for strict caution. Philip was anxious to win the goodwill of the English people. He brought with him ideas founded on a general view of European politics, and could afford to wait for ultimate success. He tried to moderate the excessive zeal of Mary for the re-establishment of the old ecclesiastical system. He did not wish that Elizabeth should seem to be a victim to the Spanish alliance. His notion was to dispose of her in marriage to some foreign prince, and so remove her from England to some place where she would be under careful supervision. The Duke of Savoy seemed a suitable husband. He had come to England in Philip's train and was dependent upon imperial protection. But before this marriage could be settled, the Duke was called to the defence of his dominions. However, if Elizabeth was to be married, she could not be kept a prisoner; and at the end of April, 1555, Bedingfield was ordered to bring her to Hampton Court. On leaving Woodstock, Elizabeth scratched with a diamond on a glass window the following lines, which express exactly her position:—

Much suspected by me:
Nothing proved can be,
Quoth Elizabeth, Prisoner

She was perhaps more frank in writing them than she intended to be. She does not deny the truth of the suspicions: the emphasis falls on the absence of proof; she rejoices in her dexterity. After all that she had gone through there was nothing definite against her. She had improved on her previous experience and could leave her prison, with her head erect.

This was not in accordance with Mary's views of the justice of the case. She believed that her sister had been disloyal; she knew that she had been adroit. She found it necessary to restore her to some semblance of favour, but she wished to do so as a matter of grace after due submission. Accordingly Elizabeth was left for a fortnight in solitude at Hampton Court, that she might feel the necessity of preferring some petition. At the end of that time she had a visit from the Chancellor, Gardiner, who requested her to make submission to the Queen, who, he had no doubt, would be good to her. Elizabeth stood to her position that nothing could be proved against her. She answered boldly that she would rather lie in prison all the days of her life; she craved no mercy, but desired the law if she had offended. The next day Gardiner returned with a message that the Queen marvelled at her stubborness: if she did not confess that she had offended, the Queen would seem to have imprisoned her wrongfully. "Nay," said Elizabeth, "it may please her to punish me as she thinketh good." "Well," answered Gardiner, "you must tell another tale before you are set at liberty." Again Elizabeth boldly declared that she would rather be in prison, with honesty and truth, than to be free and suspected by the Queen. Gardiner pointed out the result of this attitude: "Then your Grace hath the vantage of me, and the other lords, for your wrong and long imprisonment". Elizabeth affected to misunderstand the argument: "What vantage I have, you know, taking God to record I seek no vantage at your hands for your so dealing with me: but God forgive me and you also". Gardiner retired completely baffled. Elizabeth was left in solitude for a week to consider her position. Then she received a message, at ten o'clock at night, to come before the Queen. The suddenness of the summons and the lateness of the hour foretold some new disaster, and Elizabeth parted from her household, commending herself to their prayers as one who would never see them again. Sir Henry Bedingfield led her through the garden by torchlight and she was ushered into the Queen's bedroom, where Mary was seated in a chair, with all the appearance of a judge. Elizabeth knelt before her, and prayed God to preserve her, as became a true subject; she besought the Queen to regard her as such, whatever reports she might have heard against her. "You will not confess your offence," said Mary, "but stand stoutly in your truth; I pray God it may so fall out." "If it doth not," was Elizabeth's bold answer, "I request neither favour nor pardon at your Majesty's hands." "Well," said the Queen, "you stiffly still persevere in your truth. Belike you will not confess but that you have been wrongfully punished." "I must not say so, if it please your Majesty, to you." "Why, then, belike you will to others." "No," replied Elizabeth; "I have borne the burden and must bear it. I humbly beseech your Majesty to have a good opinion of me, and to think me to be your true subject, not only from the beginning hitherto, but for ever as long as life lasteth." Mary was softened. Indeed Elizabeth at this time was recognised by her enemies as having "a spirit full of incantation". Mary felt the charm of this bold, yet winsome, girl, and spoke comfortably to her. "God knows," she said in Spanish, with a sigh, as Elizabeth departed.

A few days afterwards, Bedingfield and his soldiers were withdrawn. Elizabeth was no longer in custody, but stayed quietly at Hampton Court.

It was just at this time that Mary was passing through the bitter experience of her self-deception about her pregnancy. She had mistaken for the promise of a child the signs of an incurable malady, the dropsy. She continued to hope against hope, but felt that those around her did not share her delusions. Elizabeth was the next heir to the throne. If she were set aside, the succession would be Mary of Scotland, whose French marriage made her

more dangerous to Philip than was Elizabeth. So Philip was
kindly towards her; and Mary only longed for certainty about
her religious convictions. She had little confidence in Elizabeth's
conversion to Romanism and plied her with questions. It was in
answer to such a question about transubstantiation that Elizabeth
is said to have given the famous answer:—

> *Christ was the word that spake it,*
> *He took the bread and brake it;*
> *And what His words did make it*
> *That I believe and take it.*

It was a saying the theological truth of which has become
more apparent as controversy on the point has progressed.

For a time Elizabeth continued to live at the Court, but in
October was allowed to return to her house at Hatfield, where
she gathered round her her old friends, Catherine Ashley and
Parry, and the rest. But England was unquiet; and there were
plots against Mary in which Elizabeth's household were perpetually compromised. In the middle of 1556 Sir Thomas Pope was
appointed chief officer of her household, to keep a friendly watch
over her doings. Again there were proposals for her marriage,
first to Emmanuel Philibert, Duke of Savoy, then to Eric, son of
the King of Sweden. Elizabeth refused them both, protesting that
she loved the state in which she was so much that she knew no
life to be compared with it. She was learning a formula which
afterwards stood in her good stead. She was always ready to con-
template matrimony as an ideal possibility, but always found
some reason against any particular proposal. Marriage might be
good, but not if it diminished her personal importance. Indeed,
she was at this time most careful of her popularity, and tried to
keep as large a household as she could. She lost no opportunity of
appearing in public, and steadily, but cautiously, asserted her position.

We have a picture of Elizabeth at this time, drawn by the pen
of a Venetian ambassador. It is of interest as showing how she

struck an experienced observer, and already possessed all those qualities which she afterwards displayed. "She is at present," wrote Giovanni Micheli, "of the age of twenty-three, and is esteemed to be no less fair in mind than she is in body. Albeit, in face she is pleasing rather than beautiful; but her figure is tall and well proportioned. She has a good complexion, though of a somewhat olive tint, beautiful eyes, and above all a beautiful hand, which she likes to show. She is of admirable talent and intelligence, of which she has given proof by her behaviour in the dangers and suspicions to which she has been exposed. She has great knowledge of languages, especially Italian, and for display talks nothing else with Italians. She is proud and haughty; for in spite of her mother, she holds herself as high as the Queen and equally legitimate, alleging in her own behalf that her mother would not cohabit with the King save as his wife, and that with the authority of the Church, after sentence given by the Primate of this realm; so that even if she were deceived having acted in good faith, she contracted a valid marriage and bore her child in lawful wedlock. Even supposing she be a bastard, she bears herself proudly and boastfully through her father, whom she is said to resemble more than does the Queen. Moreover, in the late King's will, she was placed on the same footing as the Queen, and was named her successor, if she died without issue. She lives on what her father bequeathed her, and is always in debt; she would be more so but that she keeps down her household not to awaken the Queen's jealousy. For there is no lord, nor knight in the kingdom, who would not enter her service, or send there his son or brother; such is the affection and love which is felt towards her. She is always pleading her poverty, in such a dexterous way as to awaken silent compassion and therefore greater affection. For every one thinks it hard that a King's daughter should be so miserably treated. Since Wyatt's rebellion she has never been free; for though she is allowed to live in her house, some twelve miles distant from London, still she has many guards and spies about her, who observe all comers and goers; and she never says or does anything that is not at once reported to the Queen. After the Queen's marriage she came to Court, and contrived to win the favour of the Spaniards, and especially of the King, with whom she is a great favourite. He has steadily opposed the Queen's desires to disinherit her by Act of Parliament or declare her illegitimate, or send her out of the kingdom. If it were not for his influence and for the fear of an insurrection, the Queen would undoubtedly find some occasion for punishing her, if not for past, at least for present, offences; for there is no conspiracy in which, justly or unjustly, her name is not mentioned and some of her servants involved. But the Queen is obliged to dissemble her dislike, and constrain herself to receive her in public with kindness and honour."

Mary's days, however, were drawing to a close. During the summer of 1558 she was ill, and in November it was plain that she was dying. Philip sent her a message advising her to recognise Elizabeth as her successor. She did so, and sent Elizabeth her last request that she would pay her personal debts, and maintain religion on the basis which she had established. The Spanish envoy who brought Philip's message, the Count de Feria, tried to impress Elizabeth with proper gratitude towards his master. She answered proudly that she owed her safety to the people of England. Then they discussed the future, and the experienced diplomatist saw that her preparations were already made. Her secretary would be Sir William Cecil, a man full of intelligence and capacity, but tainted with heresy. He saw that she would not commit herself to any one's protection, but would govern for herself. His report to his master was justified by actual facts. "To great subtlety," he wrote, "she adds very great vanity. She has heard great talk of her father's mode of action, and means to follow it. I have great fear that she thinks ill in the matter of religion, for I see that she inclines to govern by men who are suspected as heretics."

Elizabeth remained quietly at Hatfield, awaiting the news of Mary's death. She saw, day by day, new visitors arriving. Her

plans were already made, and Cecil was ready to take all necessary steps when the moment came. On November 17 the news
was brought of Mary's death; but Elizabeth was too prudent to
act in haste, and sent Sir Nicholas Throgmorton to ascertain if
the news was true. Before his return, a deputation of the Lords of
the Council arrived at Hatfield and greeted their new Queen.
Elizabeth stood for a moment irresolute. Then falling on her
knees, she exclaimed: "This is the Lord's doing, and it is mar-
vellous in our eyes".

Few rulers ever ascended a throne better prepared for her
task than did Elizabeth. The facts of her personal experience had
corresponded with the experience of the nation. Her own life had
been interwoven with the national life. She had been in imminent
danger, both under Edward and under Mary. She had suffered,
and had learned as the nation learned and suffered. She had lived
amongst perils, and had been taught the need of prudence. Self-
mastery and self-restraint had been forced upon her. Bitter experience had taught her how little she could satisfy her own desires,
how little she could confide in the wisdom or discretion of others. She had spent long hours in enforced solitude and reflection
as the drama of events passed before her. She had seen the failures
of other lives, their disappointments, and their tragic end. And, in
all this, she had been no idle spectator, but one whose own fortunes were deeply involved; and at each new turn of events men's
minds had been more closely directed to her, so that her personal
importance had been emphasised. She seemed to form part of all
that the nation had passed through. Now she was called upon to
amend the melancholy results of the ill-directed zeal of others, to
bring back England to peace and security. For all men's hopes
were set upon her as "born mere English, here among us, and
therefore most natural to us". Men looked back to the days of
Henry VIII., which loomed greater through the clouds of the
past twelve years of misgovernment, to a time when at least there
was an intelligible policy, and welcomed Elizabeth as the true inheritor of her father's spirit. Her training had been severe; but to

that severity was due the character and the qualities which enabled her to face the work which lay before her. She would not have had it otherwise, for it made her one with her people.

It would seem that, in later days, she wished for a romantic expression in art of the trials and anxieties of her early days. A portrait of her, at Hampton Court, tries to depict in allegory, which it is difficult to unfold with exactness, Elizabeth before her accession. Standing in a forest, under a tree laden with fruit, a fair young girl looks out with eyes fixed on an unknown future. On her head she bears a high white cap of Persian form, whence falls a black veil. Her right hand is placing a crown of flowers upon the head of a stag, whose head is bowed, while tears drop from its eyes. The tree's trunk is covered with inscriptions which lament the injustice of human lot. On a shield is inscribed a poem, which gives us a clue to the meaning of the whole, and celebrates the trials of Elizabeth's youth.

> *The restless swallow fits my restless mind*
> *In still reviving, still renewing, wrongs;*
> *Her just complaints of cruelty unkind*
> *Are all the music that my life prolongs.*
> *With pensive thought my weeping stag I crown;*
> *Whose melancholy tears my cares express;*
> *His tears and silence, and my sighs unknown*
> *Are all the physic that my harms redress.*
> *My only hope was in this goodly tree,*
> *Which I did plant in love, bring up in care;*
> *But all in vain, for now, too late, I see*
> *The shales be mine, the kernels others are.*
> *My music may be plaints, my physic tears*
> *If this be all the fruit my love-tree bears.*

II

PROBLEMS OF THE REIGN

꿏 While Elizabeth was exceptionally fitted to occupy the post of ruler, few rulers ever had before them a more difficult and dangerous inheritance. England under Edward VI. had been the prey of self-seeking and unscrupulous adventurers; under Mary it had been an appendage to the Spanish power. Its finances were embarrassed; it was suffering from two bad harvests; its navy was scarcely existent; its military forces were disorganised; its defences were crumbling; it had no statesmen of mark; its foreign relations were precarious. A contemporary memorandum thus puts the melancholy condition of the country: "The Queen poor; the realm exhausted; the nobles poor and decayed; good captains and soldiers wanting; the people out of order; justice not executed; the justices unmeet for their offices; all things dear; division among ourselves; war with France and Scotland; the French King bestriding the realm, having one foot in Calais and the other in Scotland; steadfast enmity, but no steadfast friendship abroad". It was difficult to know where remedy was to begin, and it was impossible to choose. The only hope lay in using wisely the opportunities offered by a new reign.

On one point of importance Elizabeth's mind was already made up. She had already selected her chief minister, and her wisdom was justified by the fidelity with which he served her for forty years. William Cecil was the son of a country gentleman who lived at Burghley, near Stamford. His father was in the service of Henry VII., and became more important under Henry VIII., when he enriched himself with the plunder of the monasteries. William was educated at Cambridge, where he married the sister of his friend Cheke, whose mother was poor and kept a small wine-shop. This imprudent marriage is the only trace of romance in Cecil's life. He did not, however, suffer for it, as his wife died in three years, and he married again the most cultivated woman of the time, Mildred Cooke, whose sister was the mother of Francis Bacon. Cecil practised at the bar till the Protector Somerset made him his secretary, and he rapidly showed a capacity for affairs. But Cecil learned prudence, and was content with scanty recognition. Under Mary he and his wife conformed to Romanism, and he was still employed in politics. How Elizabeth learned his worth we do not know; but he was preparing himself for her service and was ready at once to act in her behalf. When he took the oath as secretary, Elizabeth addressed him: "This judgment I have of you, that you will not be corrupted with any manner of gifts, and that you will be faithful to the State; and that without respect of any private will, you will give me that counsel that you think best; and if you shall know anything necessary to be declared unto me of secrecy, you shall show it to myself only, and assure yourself I will not fail to keep taciturnity therein". It was a noble expression of confidence which was well requited through a long and laborious life. A little later, the great seal was taken from the Archbishop of York and given to Sir Nicholas Bacon, Cecil's brother-in-law. The administration was to be in the hands of men who would work together.

Elizabeth's first appearance in public showed that she valued popularity above all things and spared no pains to gain it. "If ever any person had either the gift or the style to win the hearts of the people, it was this Queen; and if ever she did express the same, it was at that present, in coupling mildness with majesty, as she did, and in stately stooping to the meanest sort. All her faculties were in motion, and every motion seemed a well-guided action. Her eye was set on one; her ear listened to another; her judgment ran upon a third; to a fourth she addressed her speech; her spirit seemed to be everywhere, and yet so entire in herself, as it seemed to be nowhere else. Some she pitied; some she commended; some she thanked; at others she pleasantly and wittily jested, contemning no person, neglecting no office; and distributing her smiles, looks and graces so artificially that thereupon the people redoubled the testimony of their joys, and afterwards raising everything to the highest strain, filled the ears of all men with immoderate extolling their prince." In all the pageantry which ushers in a new reign, Elizabeth was busy in endearing herself to the hearts of her people, she used every opportunity of showing herself in public, and she was affable to all. She laid from the beginning the foundations of that personal popularity which she never lost, and which was her strongest weapon amid all her perils.

Yet there were serious questions to be faced, which needed settlement; and foremost among them was the question of religion. In nothing was the legacy of the last two reigns more disastrous, as they represented periods of reaction which had checked the natural development of the reforming process begun under Henry VIII. Henry had abolished the Papal jurisdiction and had suppressed the monasteries, which no longer fulfilled any useful function. The system and services of the Church were simplified according to the requirements of the New Learning and the increased intelligence of the people; and the process thus begun was to go on slowly adjusting the old system to the national capacity. There were some minds which were imbued with the principles of the more thorough-going changes wrought on the Continent; and under Edward VI., these principles were caught at by adventurers, chiefly to give them an opportunity for further pillage of ecclesiastical property. The result of their action was to alarm the moderate men, who had been the chief supporters and advisers of Henry VIII. They were driven back upon the old system, and welcomed Mary, who was a devoted adherent to the Papacy. Under her, Gardiner strove to undo what he had done before; and the zeal of those who with him tried to go back upon their past was fierce and indiscreet. England unwillingly accepted the Papal restoration and the Spanish alliance. Its rulers laboured to force all men into rigid uniformity and close the mouths of gainsayers.

The fires of Smithfield filled England with horror; and Mary's reign ended amid gloom and disaster. The revival of Romanism was associated with all that England felt to be most repressive of its energies. Elizabeth, as the daughter of Anne Boleyn, was heir to the problems of the Reformation. Great as they might be, they were not so great or so dangerous as those connected with the maintenance of the old system.

The object which Elizabeth had in view was, first of all, to allay, as much as might be, the animosities which had been engendered in the previous time. Mary's bishops had been appointed from those who had suffered under Edward VI., and as a body were bound to maintain the Roman system. On the other hand, those divines who had most strongly expressed reforming opinions, fled before the Marian persecution, and lived on the Continent. They now returned home strong adherents of the system of Calvin and almost fanatically opposed to anything which savoured of Papacy. It was impossible to bring these two extremes into agreement; it was inevitable that some should be discontented. But the great bulk of the English people wished for a national Church, independent of Rome, with simple services, not too unlike those to which they had been accustomed. It was important that the Papal jurisdiction should be definitely ended, and that, at the same time, the framework of the Church should be retained; provided that these two objects were secured there should be large liberty for theological discussion. What was needed was a system which would supply an expression for the religious consciousness of the nation, and would allow of freedom within the limits of ecclesiastical order. After a time, it was hoped that transient animosities would cease and reason and moderation would prevail.

As a first step towards carrying out this policy, a proclamation was issued forbidding mutual recriminations, and ordering that no changes in public worship should be made without authority. Soon the Epistles and Gospels were allowed to be read in English as well as the Litany. Public preaching was prohibited lest men's minds should be inflamed by strong language. These steps were so significant that Archbishop Heath refused to crown a Queen whose acts were so ambiguous; and Elizabeth was crowned by Oglethorpe, Bishop of Carlisle, on January 15, 1559. Ten days afterwards, Elizabeth opened her first Parliament, and the policy of the new reign was declared by Sir Nicholas Bacon. The Queen's desire, he said, was "to unite the people of the realm in one uniform order"; for this purpose they were to "eschew contumelious and opprobrious words as heretic, schismatic and Papist". They were to make such laws as might "tend to the establishment of God's Church and the tranquillity of the realm," avoiding what might "breed idolatry and superstition," yet "taking heed by no licentious or loose handling to give occasion for contempt or irreverence". Laws were necessary also for reforming the civil order of the realm, and repairing the losses and decays which the Crown had suffered. Calais was lost; trade was stopped; the coasts were unprotected. They must consider the need of self-preservation. The Queen assured them that she was not "wedded to her own fantasy, nor for any private affection would quarrel with foreign princes," nothing was so dear to her as the goodwill of her people.

When business began, the Acts necessary for the severance of the English Church from Rome were quickly introduced. First fruits were restored to the Crown. The proposal to restore the royal supremacy raised opposition from the Bishops. It was, however, a remarkable fact that never had that body been so numerically weak. The Metropolitan See of Canterbury was vacant by the death of Pole, who died at the same time as Mary. Nine other Bishops had died within the previous year, and their sees had not been filled up. Of the remainder, some were ill, so that not more than ten were present in the House of Lords. Their opposition was unavailing; but it was necessary to silence them before proceeding to change of ritual. They were accordingly bidden to argue against theologians of a different opinion, in the presence of the Lords and Commons, the subjects of (1) the use

of prayer in an unknown tongue; (2) the right of national
Churches to ordain their own rites and ceremonies; (3) the sacrifice of the Mass. The controversy began on March 31, on the
understanding that the Bishops were to speak first and their ad-
versaries were to reply. This method did not satisfy the Bishops
and, after two days, they refused to proceed. Indeed the disputa-
tion was merely an empty show; but the refusal to continue was
regarded as contempt. Two of the Bishops were committed to
the Tower; the rest were under bail to appear when called for.

After this the "Act for Restoring to the Crown the Ancient
Jurisdiction over the State ecclesiastical and spiritual" was
passed. But Elizabeth refused the title of "Supreme Head of the
Church," and substituted for it "Supreme Governor as well in
spiritual and ecclesiastical causes as temporal". She had a conception of her own of the independence of the Church; and,
desirous as she was of power, she would not accept it where
it was not rightly hers. She explained the practical meaning of the
title to the Spanish ambassador: "she did not intend to be called
Head of the Church, but she could not let her subjects' money be
carried out of the realm by the Pope any more". Meanwhile a
Commission had been sitting for revising the Prayer Book of Edward VI. When their work was done, the "Act for Uniformity
of Common Prayer" was passed and the ecclesiastical change was
legally complete. England was again independent. Its Church was
again free to work out its own problems. Its system has not
changed from that day to this.

Perhaps in nothing was Elizabeth's foresight more conspicuous than in her ecclesiastical policy. She had a clear conception of
the nature of the Church, and was careful never to interfere with
its independence. In this she was almost alone. Her ministers
might take a political view of the matter; the Queen saw further
than mere policy. Her definition of the royal supremacy reserved
the freedom of the Church within the necessary sphere of allegiance to the State. It avoided collisions, but recognised spiritual
authority. Elizabeth was anxious that the Church should manage

its own affairs. On many occasions she declined to interfere in difficulties and refused to allow Parliament to interfere. She maintained the authority of the Bishops and rated it higher than they did themselves. She was willing to wait for the reformed system to take root and was content to guard it in its beginnings.

In England generally the religious settlement was welcomed by the people and corresponded to their wish. The English were not greatly interested in theological questions. They detested the Pope; they wished for services which they could understand, and were weary of superstition. The number of staunch Romanists or strong Protestants was very small. The clergy were prepared to acquiesce in the change. Out of 9400 clergy in England, only 192 refused the oath of supremacy.[1] Amongst these were all the Bishops, except Kitchin of Llandaff. Some of them fled abroad; others were committed to the Tower and afterwards to private custody. There was some difficulty in filling up the vacant sees, owing to the unwillingness of Matthew Parker to accept the Archbishopric of Canterbury. Parker was a man admirably fitted for the post. He had been chaplain to Anne Boleyn, Master of Corpus College, Cambridge, and Dean of Lincoln. During Mary's reign he had lived quietly in hiding. He was known to Cecil as a man of great learning, of genuine piety and uprightness. He had never been a partisan, and was untouched by the theology of Geneva or the theological quarrels of the Marian exiles. He was the man above all others to exercise a wise and moderating influence. At last his objections were overcome, and he was consecrated on December 17. In a short time the other sees were filled, and the momentous change was accomplished.

The change did not produce much disturbance in England itself, but it seriously affected England's position in Europe, where the dividing line in politics was between Catholic and Protestant. If Elizabeth began her measures cautiously, it was because her eye was carefully fixed on Philip II., who was her only ally, and whose pronounced hostility would have been fatal. England was

[1] See note, p. 58.

at war with France and must make peace in company with Spain. Philip wished to maintain his alliance with England; but he could not be the ally of an heretical Power. So anxious was he to check Elizabeth in her religious changes that, in January, 1559, he made her an offer of his hand. Elizabeth did not at once refuse, and paused for a time; but, after a month's reflection, she declined the offer saying that the Pope would not allow her to marry her brother-in-law, and that her people were strong enough to maintain their liberties at home and abroad. Really, she had come to the conclusion that Philip would be compelled reluctantly to stand by her, whatever she did, through dread of increasing the power of France. Great as might be his attachment to the Papacy, his ancestral animosity to France was still greater. If Elizabeth were removed, her successor on the English throne would be Mary of Scotland, who was married to the Dauphin. It was better that England should be under an heretical Queen, who was under obligations to Spain, than that it should be an appanage of the French monarchy. Elizabeth felt that with a little dexterity she could drag Philip in her train. In the conference for peace France failed to sow distrust between England and Spain. The peace was concluded in April; but England had to endure the loss of Calais, though it obtained from France a recognition of Elizabeth's right to the Crown.

Elizabeth's first Parliament did not end without raising the question of the Queen's marriage. The Commons waited upon her at Whitehall, and the Speaker set forth their desire that the succession to the Throne should be firmly established. Elizabeth answered in one of those speeches for which she became famous —a gracious acceptance of the request and an enunciation of great principles and admirable intentions, without committing herself to anything—a speech which pleased the ear and won the confidence, without enlightening the understanding, of the hearers. She would live for her people; she would trust in Providence; she would decide for the best; provision should be made for a successor in God's good time; her children, if she had any, might turn out ill. "As for me," she ended, "it shall be sufficient that a marble stone shall declare that a Queen, having lived and reigned so many years, died a virgin." Thus, from the first, she adopted the line of conduct which stood her in good stead. Marriage was an open question; any particular alliance must be proved to be for the nation's good; she had no wishes of her own. Thus her hand was a bait which might be dangled before the eyes of political aspirants; but Elizabeth knew that, if it were once swallowed, it was lost for ever. She loved power too much to give up any part of what she possessed. She was determined to make her position as a woman a help, rather than a hindrance, to her politics as a ruler. So, after refusing Philip, Elizabeth admitted the suit of his near relative, the Archduke Charles, son of the Emperor Ferdinand. She received his portrait with every sign of delight and hung it at the foot of her bed. She sent a list of inquiries to be made about him—his age, stature, height, fatness, strength, complexion, studies, education, temper and the like—asking even "Whether he had been noted to have loved any woman, and in what kind?" At the same time, Eric, son of Gustavus Vasa, King of Sweden, sent his brother to England to plead his cause, and wrote in terms of devoted affection, asking for some "little writing" declaring her feelings towards him. Meanwhile Elizabeth was relieving herself by carrying on a flirtation with Lord Robert Dudley, which sorely perturbed her ministers. We have a description of her, in her galley, with the imperial ambassador, the Duke of Finland, and Lord Robert Dudley below—all engaged in trying to win her attention. No wonder Cecil sadly wrote: "Here is a great resort of wooers and controversy among lovers. Would to God the Queen had one, and the rest honourably satisfied."

There was still another claimant for Elizabeth's hand whom Cecil secretly favoured. In his eyes, the great danger to Elizabeth's throne came from the union between France and Scotland. Despite the stipulation of the peace of Cateau Cambresis, the Dauphiness Mary assumed the arms of England. The sudden death of Henry II., in July, set her husband Francis II. on the French throne, and the management of affairs fell into the hands of his wife's kinsfolk, the Guises, whose plan was to sweep out heresy and unite Scotland and England with France. Scotland was ruled by the Queen-Regent, Mary of Guise, with the help of the French troops. On the Scottish side, England was always vulnerable, as the chronic warfare which prevailed along the Borders could at any moment become serious. The Warden of the Marches wrote that the men of Teviotdale pillaged at will: "We be able nothing to withstand the enemy's power, they being of so great force and we so weak". This was serious in view of French hostility, and some steps were necessary to secure the defences of the border. One method, which might be pursued with caution, was to incite the Scottish Protestants to rise against the Regent, and Sir Ralph Sadler was sent to Berwick with instructions to "nourish faction between Scots and French". It was, however, a dangerous matter for the English Queen to stir up rebellion in Scotland, especially if the rebellion were unsuccessful. The Protestant nobles tried to find some plausible reason for invoking Elizabeth's intervention, and at last discovered a substantial guarantee. James Hamilton, Duke of Châtelherault, had been Regent till he was ousted by the Queen: he would make over his claims to his son, the Earl of Arran; the French were then to be expelled, Mary's claims to the Crown disannulled, and Arran married to Elizabeth. So, in August, Arran came secretly to London and was hidden in Cecil's house, where Elizabeth saw him, but soon decided that he was no match for her, though, as usual, she did not say so.

It was hard for Elizabeth to decide what course to pursue towards Scottish affairs. It was dangerous to risk a war with France, in which Philip warned her he could not take part. Moreover, Elizabeth was entirely opposed to the principles on which the Scottish Lords were acting; she wished to be rid of Mary's claims on England, but she did not wish to help the Lords of the Congregation. The Calvinistic doctrine of election led to the consequence that princes who acted contrary to God's will ought to be deposed. The Scots claimed, in fact, the right of judging the title and character of their ruler—a claim to which Elizabeth's doubtful legitimacy made her doubly sensitive. How could she object to Spain or France fomenting insurrection in England if she gave help to the rebels in Scotland? So Elizabeth long hesitated, and was moved only by the persistence of Cecil, who wrote "that as the proceeding for removing the French out of Scotland does not please Her Majesty, he may, with her favour, be spared intermeddling therein. In any other service, whether in kitchen or garden, he is ready from the bottom of his heart to serve her to his life's end." Elizabeth was moved by Cecil's representations; but she made her own reflections. She knew that, though her ministers might advise her, she had to bear the ultimate responsibility for her actions, and that her reputation was in her own keeping only. She also knew that the foremost desire of those who served her was to secure themselves against the possibility of Mary's accession, which would inevitably mean the loss of their heads. She concluded that some amount of uncertainty on this point was not undesirable, as it guaranteed their unswerving fidelity. She saw the desirability of using the opportunity for causing the chief men in England to commit themselves as opponents of Mary's succession; and she grasped the need of caution.

So Elizabeth set to work to play a game which bewildered every one. She adopted a more than feminine irresoluteness, and carried it into diplomacy with astonishing assurance. There was no truth nor honesty in anything she said. At the end of the year she sent Sir Nicholas Throgmorton to France with instructions: "If they shall ask whether she means to aid the Scots or no, he may assure them that at his departure hence no such thing was meant". She wrote to the Regent of Scotland that "all the foundation of all her doings was laid upon honour and truth, which she esteems above all things". At the same time, she sent ships to Berwick, with orders to the admiral that "he might provoke a quarrel, if he did not find one". No wonder that the Spanish ambassador wrote of her: "This woman is possessed with a hundred thousand devils; and yet she pretends to me that she would like to be a nun, and live in a cell, and tell her beads from morning to night".

When Elizabeth at last made up her mind to help the Scots, she contrived, by much pressure, to induce the Duke of Norfolk to take command of the troops which she sent to the Borders. He was the premier Duke in England, a young man of no great ability as a commander; but it was worth while to associate him directly with a course of action which was in itself somewhat discreditable. When military operations were begun, the Scots tried to throw all the burden on their allies. The French reinforcements were dispersed by a gale in the Channel, and the English fleet blockaded Leith while it was besieged by land. The military operations were inglorious, and Leith surrendered only through famine and in consequence of the death of the Regent. In June both sides were ready to treat, and Cecil was sent as the English Commissioner. He had suffered much from the Queen's ill humour as she watched the slow success of the English arms. "I have had such a torment with the Queen's Majesty as an ague hath not in five fits so much abated me," he sadly wrote in May. The war was his doing, and he was held responsible for the result; he was sent to win all that he could. On July 6, 1560, the treaty was signed at Edinburgh. It provided for the withdrawal of the French troops from Scotland and the appointment of a Council of twelve nobles, appointed partly by the Scottish Queen and partly by the Parliament. Further, it was agreed that "since the Kingdoms of England and Ireland rightly belonged to the serene Elizabeth, therefore the King and Queen Mary shall abstain from using the title and insignia of these realms for all future time".

These were substantial advantages which Cecil brought back. Elizabeth's right to the Crown was admitted by France; her relations with the Scots nobles were condoned, their claim to a share in the Government was granted; and the threat of a hostile invasion from the Borders was removed. But Elizabeth clamoured for more, and expressed herself dissatisfied. She counted the money which the war had cost and demanded substantial returns in payment of an indemnity. The state of her finances at her accession impressed upon her the need of strict economy and careful management. She had sent to Antwerp Sir Thomas Gresham, who consolidated outstanding loans, reduced the interest, restored England's credit, and bought cannon and ammunition, which he secretly shipped to England. At home, the Queen diminished her household expenditure to a third of what it had been under Mary. She revived the military spirit of the Londoners and was present at the drill of the train-bands in St. James's Park, mounted on a Neapolitan courser. There were signs of a new England coming into being; but it would be helped on by strict frugality rather than by great undertakings. Elizabeth grudged every penny that she spent, and judged of military operations by their cost. So when Cecil came back he was told by his friends that "no better service had ever been done to England," and that "the Queen could not have bought it too dearly". But Elizabeth showed him no gratitude, either for his wise counsel or for his skilful diplomacy. She even left him to pay the expenses of his journey, which sorely embarrassed him.

Cecil was greatly downcast, for he saw the Queen pursuing a course which he regarded as disastrous; he saw her abandoning the counsel of her experienced advisers for that of Lord Robert Dudley, whom she treated with a familiarity that set all men's tongues wagging. Robert Dudley was the son of John, Duke of Northumberland, who had perished on the scaffold for his plot against Queen Mary. During the period of his father's power, under Edward IV., Robert had been known to Elizabeth. He was of the same age, and she admired him even as a boy "for his goodly person". At the age of eighteen he married Amy, daughter of Sir John Robsart, a Norfolk gentleman of good property. He was committed to the Tower with his father, and was a captive at the same time as Elizabeth. After his release he did good service in the campaign against France, and fought in the battle of St. Quentin. On Elizabeth's accession he was made Master of the Horse and a member of the Council. He was conspicuous in tournaments and other festivities of the Court, and the Queen's personal affection for him was undisguised. The foreign ambassadors in England had no real belief in the marriage projects which they submitted to the Queen. As early as April, 1559, Feria wrote: "They tell me that she is enamoured of my Lord Robert Dudley and will never let him leave her side. He is in such favour that people say that she visits him in his chamber day and night. Nay, it is even reported that his wife has a cancer on the breast, and that the Queen waits only till she die to marry him." We know nothing of Dudley's married life. There is no reason for thinking it unhappy, save that his wife did not accompany him to Court, but lived for the most part in the country, moving from place to place, where no one seemed to trouble themselves about her existence, as they watched the growth of Dudley's greatness. In January, 1560, De Quadra spoke of him as "the King that is to be. There is not a man who does not cry out on him and her with indignation. She tells me that the Scots expect her to marry the Earl of Arran as a condition of the union. She will as little marry Arran as she will the Archduke; she will marry none but the favoured Robert." Hence it was that Cecil left the Court with a heavy heart, for his departure left the field open for Dudley, whom he knew to be empty-headed, self-seeking, and incapable of any lofty purpose. De Quadra wrote of him with great outspokenness: "Lord Robert is the worst young fellow I ever encountered. He is heartless, spiritless, treacherous, and false." His object was to follow in his father's steps and make himself ruler of England by controlling the Queen. For this purpose Cecil's influence must be overthrown. Cecil was working for the union of Scotland and England by a marriage of the Queen with Arran: Dudley opposed a project which would have deprived him of his power. So, when Cecil came back form Scotland, he received neither gratitude for his services nor payment for his expenses, while Dudley was all-powerful and had just been granted a privilege, remunerative to himself, but dangerous to the public finances, of exporting woollen goods free of duty. Cecil was so downcast that he thought of resigning office, when an unexpected event made a new call on his loyalty, and brought his enemy to his feet.

This event was the sudden death of Dudley's wife. She was living at Cumnor Place, in Oxfordshire, in a house rented by Antony Forster, her husband's steward. On Sunday, September 8, she gave her servants leave to go to the fair at Abingdon. She dined alone with a lady living in the neighbourhood. When the servants returned home late in the evening they found their mistress lying at the bottom of a staircase with her neck broken.

When this news reached Windsor, where Dudley was in attendance on the Queen, they both felt that it exposed them to grave suspicions. Their familiarity was a matter of common talk; and Dudley's ambitious projects were scarcely concealed. Dudley's wife was obviously an obstacle in his way. It had been said that he would divorce her. Cecil, in his bitter mortification, had told the Spanish ambassador that Dudley would soon remove her by poison. A few days after this gloomy prophecy came the news of her death. What could be more clear than that she had been made away with? Dudley seems to have thought that his wisest course was to court full inquiry and to take no part in it himself. He did not go to Cumnor, but sent his cousin to see that an inquest was held and the truth fully discovered. Two investigations were held, apparently with all possible care; but nothing could be discovered about the cause of the mishap, and a verdict was returned of "accidental death". The most probable conclusion is that Lady Amy's forlorn condition preyed upon her mind. "She had been heard many times to pray God to deliver her from desperation." The loneliness and darkness of the night, the empty house, may have suggested to her a means of ending a life which was a burden to herself and others. In a sudden fit of despair she opened the door and flung herself down the winding staircase. Dudley was not guilty of scheming her murder—indeed, the means adopted was too clumsy to have been deliberate—but he must have felt that he was guilty of gross neglect and utter disregard of one whom he was bound to cherish. It is no wonder that he did not venture to attend the funeral of one who in a very real sense had been his victim.

The result of this tragedy was the restoration of Cecil's power. Dudley put himself at once in Cecil's hands, as the only man who could advise him. "I pray you," he wrote, "let me hear from you what you think best for me to do. If you doubt, I pray you ask the question, for the sooner you can advise me thither the more I shall thank you. I am sorry so sudden a chance should breed me so great a change: for methinks I am here all this while as it were in a dream, and far—too far—from the place I am bound to be." It was tacitly understood that Cecil was to do his best to repair the scandal. Of course Elizabeth's enemies had no doubt of Dudley's guilt or of Elizabeth's connivance. Mary Stuart, in France, laughed and said: "The Queen of England is about to marry her horsekeeper, who has killed his wife to make room for her". Throgmorton sent his secretary from Paris to ask Elizabeth what he was to say. She looked ill and harassed and could only refer him to the verdict at the inquest: "It fell out as should touch neither his honesty nor her honour". Elizabeth, as she looked back upon the past, must have seen that she was repeating a former experience. She had endangered herself before by a coarse flirtation with Seymour: now there was no one to call her to account, but she was endangering her position by an unseemly flirtation with Dudley. Doubtless she saw her folly and regretted it; but she was too proud to avow her regret, or to reverse her conduct suddenly. Still her eyes were open to the fact that she was derided abroad and had sown discontent at home. In the beginning of October she told Cecil "that she had made up her mind and did not intend to marry Lord Robert"; yet she did not break off her intimacy with him. Her treatment of him varied with her moods. She proposed to make him a peer, but when the patent was brought for her signature she cut it in pieces with a knife, saying that "the Dudleys had been traitors through three descents".

When Dudley remonstrated, she "clapped him on the cheeks with 'No, no, the bear and the ragged staff is not so soon over-thrown'". Some of the old nobles were of opinion that if the Queen would marry any one and bear children, it would be "the readiest way, with the help of God, to bring us a blessed Prince which shall redeem us out of thraldom". When, on this ground, they urged her to marry Dudley, she would "pup with her lips and say she could not marry a subject".

Political dangers for a time checked Elizabeth in her folly. France had not been able to interfere in Scotland, because the Huguenots, helped by Elizabeth's emissaries, had risen against the Guises. By the end of the year they were overcome, and the Guises were again triumphant. France refused to ratify the Treaty of Edinburgh on the ground that "a treaty made by sub-jects without the consent of their Sovereign was void". The French Queen continued to bear the arms of England, and a re-newal of warfare seemed imminent, when on December 5 Francis II. died and Mary was left a widow.

France was no longer under the power of the Guises, and for a moment Elizabeth dreamed of using the opportunity to secure her personal happiness at the expense of England's welfare. She allowed Dudley to propose to De Quadra, the Spanish ambassa-dor, that Philip should urge his marriage with the Queen, on con-dition that England returned to its old allegiance to the Pope. His own desires were purely personal; he wished to marry the Queen, and was annoyed to find that the Anglican clergy preached against the marriage. He would show them that, if they opposed his plans, he could turn elsewhere; and Elizabeth allowed his project to proceed. She discussed it in February with De Quadra; she told him, what he already knew, that "she was no angel"; she had not made up her mind to marry Dudley, though she saw in him many excellent qualities; but every day she felt the want of a husband: she would do nothing without Philip's sanction.

Luckily Philip delayed in answering, and Cecil contrived to get the negotiation into his hand. Just at this time a practical question arose, the answer to which affected the position of the English Church. Pope Pius IV. was engaged in summoning a Council to Trent, and a nuncio was on his way to invite England to send representatives. By England's answer to this request Philip could judge of Elizabeth's sincerity. The proposal was beset with difficulties. On the one side, the English Church was a part of the Catholic Church; and, in Cecil's words, "could not refuse to allow the presidency of the Pope, provided it was understood that the Pope was not above the Council, but merely its head; and its decision should be accepted in England if they were in harmony with Holy Scripture and the first four Councils". On the other side, could the Pope accept this position? Could he recognise the English Bishops, who had abjured his supremacy, but, as Cecil pointed out, "had been apostolically ordained, and not merely elected by a congregation like Lutheran or Calvinist heretics?" It was impossible to suppose that the Pope was prepared to recognise the constitution of the English Church; if he did not, the coming of the nuncio would only stir up discontent. So the answer was given that England could not receive the nuncio; it would send representatives to a free and really General Council, not to a Council where no man's voice would be heard "but such as were already sworn to the maintenance of the Pope's authority". When this answer was given on May 5, 1561, Dudley's intrigue disappeared; though, a month later, De Quadra writes that he was in a barge on the Thames, with the Queen and Dudley, "when they began to talk nonsense, and went so far that Lord Robert said, as I was on the spot, there was no reason why they should not be married, if the Queen pleased. She said that perhaps I did not understand sufficient English." Certainly, at this period, Elizabeth allowed gross folly to lead her to the furthest point of wilfulness, and only in extremities fell back reluctantly on common sense and public duty.

It was the question of her relation to Mary Stuart which restored Elizabeth to prudence. Probably opinions will always differ about the causes of the life-long hostility between the Queens, and how far it was inevitable. It is certain that Elizabeth regarded Mary from the first as her chief enemy. She had warred in Scotland that she might secure from Mary the recognition of her right to the English Crown. Mary answered that she could not ratify the terms of the Treaty of Edinburgh, because they might be construed as a resignation of her right to be Elizabeth's heir. Elizabeth refused all friendship till the treaty was ratified, would not allow Mary to pass through England on her way to Scotland in August, and even sent the English fleet to intercept her. From the day that Mary landed in Scotland till her death the two Queens stood in constant rivalry and waged a never-ending war. At first Elizabeth's unyielding attitude combined the Scots in Mary's favour, and Elizabeth was pressed to acknowledge her right of succession.

Indeed, the question of the succession was pressing on many sides, and Elizabeth's objection to face it was beset with many difficulties. In August, 1561, great scandal was caused in the country by the discovery that Lady Catharine Grey was with child. Lady Catharine was the sister of Lady Jane Grey, and, according to the will of Henry VIII., was the next heir to the throne. She declared that she had been secretly married to the Earl of Hertford, eldest son of the Protector Somerset. It was clear that this clandestine marriage was the result of a political combination and had been contracted at a time when Elizabeth's flirtation with Dudley seemed likely to end in a marriage. The strong Protestants and the personal enemies of Dudley had combined to have a leader in the revolution which was expected to follow on the Queen's marriage with Dudley. Lady Catharine and her husband were sent to the Tower, and an attempt was made to discover who were privy to the marriage, which was declared invalid, as no witnesses were produced. It was soon found that many important persons had knowledge of it, and further inquiry was dropped. But Elizabeth wreaked her wrath on Catharine and her husband, who were kept rigorously in prison. By bribing their keepers they occasionally managed to meet, and Catharine bore another child. Elizabeth's anger increased, and Hertford was fined £15,000 for his offences. In vain Catharine pleaded forgiveness. During an outbreak of plague she was allowed to leave her prison for an uncle's house, but was again committed and only left the Tower again to die in 1567.

The discovery of this intrigue made Elizabeth more anxious to come to terms with Mary, and arrangements were made for a meeting between the two Queens. But Elizabeth was soon disturbed by another discovery. The Earl of Lennox, who had married the daughter of Margaret, sister of Henry VIII., had long been resident in England, where his wife held a high position. It appeared that Lady Lennox was trying to make herself leader of the Romanist party and was scheming to marry her son, Lord Darnley, to the Scottish Queen, so that "he should be King both of Scotland and England". Lady Lennox was committed to the Tower; but her plan was found to have a number of adherents and betokened danger.

Whatever might have been Elizabeth's intentions with regard to Mary, they were changed by the aspect of affairs in France, where war had again broken out and the Guises were again regaining power. Their victory would be the signal for a rising in England, and Elizabeth could not afford to take any steps which would strengthen Mary's position as leader of the English Romanists. To check the Guises, Elizabeth sent help to their opponents, but even then she made it plain that her real desire was to secure English interests by occupying Dieppe and Havre as guarantees for the restoration of Calais. But the Huguenots were defeated, and in the pacification which followed England received nothing. The Earl of Warwick vainly endeavoured to hold Havre against the French forces. A plague broke out among the English garrison; and there were sad complaints of mismanagement in sending out military supplies. "The cast-iron pieces were waste and unserviceable; there was want of stocks, axle-trees and wheels; they were short of ramrods by one half; the carpenters sent out were utterly ignorant of their art; the shot was utterly destroyed; there were no bowstrings or arrows." Warwick was driven to evacuate Havre in July, 1563, and the expedition ended in complete disaster.

Parliament, which met at the beginning of the year, showed its temper by passing an "Act for the Assurance of the Queen's Power over all Estates," which made all who upheld the Pope's authority or jurisdiction liable to the penalties of præmunire, and imposed the oath of Supremacy on all holders of office, lay or spiritual, in the realm. It further urged the Queen's marriage and the settlement of the succession. As a sample of Elizabeth's oratory, the speech with which she dismissed Parliament may be quoted:—

"The two petitions that you presented me, in many words expressed, contained these two things in sum, as of your cares the greatest—my marriage and my succession—of which two, the last, I think, is best to be touched; and of the other, a silent thought may serve; for I had thought it had been so desired as none other tree's blossoms should have been minded ere hope of my fruit had been denied you. But to the last, think not that you had needed this desire, if I had seen a time so fit, and it so ripe to be denounced. The greatness of the cause, therefore, and need of your returns doth make me say that which I think the wise may easily guess—that as a short time for so long a continuance ought not to pass by rote, as many telleth tales, even so as cause by conference with the learned shall show me matter worthy utterance for your behoof, so shall I more gladly pursue your good, after my days, than with my prayers be a means to linger my living thread. . . . I hope I shall die in quiet with a *Nunc Dimittis*, which cannot be without I see some glimpse of your following after my graved bones. And, by the way, if any doubt that I am as it were by vow or determination bent never to trade that life, put out that heresy; your belief is awry—for as I think it best for a private woman, so do I strive with myself to think it not most meet for a prince—and if I can bend my will to your need, I will not resist such a mind."

Surely perverse ingenuity could not go further in the discovery of ambiguous utterance. The members of Parliament must have retired in bewilderment.

However, Elizabeth, by this time, seems to have made up her mind that marriage with Dudley was impossible, and that any marriage would really weaken her position. It is very probable that she believed she would be childless; and a marriage without issue would necessitate a settlement of the succession. With a husband on one side and a recognised successor on the other, her own position would be much weaker. Her strength lay in the uncertainty about the future, which bound all her followers to a personal loyalty of unswerving devotion. As it was, the interests of all who were concerned in making the new England were necessarily bound up with the maintenance of Elizabeth's throne. Why should she, by any act of hers, alter this? Uncertainty about the future might perplex her people; but was any certainty within reach which would give them greater hope? With an imperious fatalism the Queen resolved to keep what she had and leave the future to care for itself. She met each separate proposal for her marriage with dexterity, and, without declaring any fixed intention, allowed it to pass away. She was always willing to entertain proposals, but always found some fatal flaw. She wished to educate England to look to herself alone. Experience also had taught her that it was safest to stand by herself. Doubtless she was attracted to Dudley by his physical charms, and she allowed herself to enjoy his companionship in her idle hours. Perhaps she thought that by marrying a subject she would be more free than if she married a foreign prince. She was too acute not to see through Dudley's ambition, and she was too greedy of power not to see how much she would lose by sharing it with anyone. She keenly watched the growth of Dudley's assumption of authority, when he felt secure of her favour. She delighted in reminding him of his dependence. When he presumed, she put him to open shame. Thus, in the height of his power, he resented that one of his followers was refused admission to the Privy Chamber by the usher, who had his orders about the quality of those who were to enter. Dudley turned upon him, angrily called him a knave, and said that he should not continue long in his office. The usher stepped in before Dudley, and kneeling before the Queen, told her what had occurred and asked her pleasure. Elizabeth turned furiously on Dudley: "God's death, my Lord, I have wished you well, but my favour is not so locked up for you that others shall not partake thereof; for I have many servants, unto whom I have, and will at my pleasure, bequeath my favour and likewise reserve the same. And, if you think to rule here, I will take a course to see you forthcoming. I will have here but one mistress, and no master." This rebuke, we are not surprised to hear, so quelled Dudley "that his feigned humility was long after one of his best virtues". In fact, Elizabeth discovered the advantages to be gained by combining the parts of the woman and the Queen. As Queen, she could administer reproofs in public; as woman she could forgive in private. Her real gratification lay in receiving homage; and the homage of an aspiring suitor was more certain than even that of a dependent and submissive husband.

When Elizabeth had made up her mind, so far as her mind was ever made up, as regards herself, she could afford to interest herself in Mary's marriage projects. Mary wished to marry Don Carlos or the Archduke Charles of Austria, and so increase her political influence. Elizabeth informed her that if she married into the Royal House of Spain, France or Austria, she would regard her as an enemy; if she chose a Protestant prince or a French noble she would name her as her successor. A little later she proposed that Mary should marry an English nobleman, or some other great person of another realm, "not of such greatness as suspicion might be gathered that he might intend trouble to the realm". At last, with an air of one who makes a supreme sacrifice, she suggested Lord Robert Dudley. How far Elizabeth was sincere in making this proposal cannot be determined. It is just possible that she trusted in Dudley's devotion to herself to avoid the dangers which might beset her if Mary was recognised as her successor. It is also possible that she made a proposal, which she knew that Mary would bitterly resent, in the hopes of goading her to take a step which would make her recognition impossible. Either result would be an immediate gain. Perhaps she chose to invent a position which admitted of alternative issues.

While she awaited the results of this suggestion, Elizabeth, in August, 1564, paid a visit to Cambridge, that she might solace her mind in that ancient seat of learning, and find some relief from her perplexities by captivating the youthful enthusiasm of its students. Cecil, as Chancellor, with his usual carefulness, supervised every detail of the ceremonial to be observed. On August 5 the Queen entered Cambridge by Newnham Mill, where she was received by the Mayor and Corporation. Then she proceeded to King's College, along a line of students and masters, marshalled in order. At the west door of the chapel she was welcomed by the inevitable orator, to whose Latin speech she listened carefully, shaking her head in deprecation of his praises, and sometimes expressing her modesty in articulate Latin. When he praised the unmarried life, she said: "God's blessing of thine heart; there continue". When he had finished, she said "that she would answer him again in Latin, but for fear she should speak false Latin, and then he would laugh at her". Then she passed into the chapel, where a stately service was sung.

The Queen lodged in King's College; and, on the next day, which was a Sunday, attended service at the University Church, walking under a canopy carried by the four senior doctors. After evensong the "Aulularia" of Plautus was acted in King's College Chapel, and the performance was not over till midnight. On the following day the University lectures and disputations were resumed, and the Queen was present as an interested onlooker. In the evening a play, on the somewhat inappropriate subject of "Dido," was provided for her amusement. On the following day Elizabeth visited the various Colleges, being greeted at each by a Latin speech, and receiving a volume of Latin and Greek verses composed in her honour by members of the College. Returning to her lodging, "as Her Grace rode through the street, she talked much with divers scholars in Latin". The last day of her stay in Cambridge was devoted to an academic ceremonial. The most learned doctors were chosen to dispute on two significant conclusions: "That the authority of Scripture is greater than that of the Church," and that "The civil magistrate has authority in ecclesiastical matters". When these had been satisfactorily proved, the Duke of Norfolk and Lord Robert Dudley knelt before the Queen and "humbly desired her to speak something to the University, and in Latin". At first she affected coyness and asked that she might speak in English. Cecil reminded her that the University always used Latin as its official language. Elizabeth asked Cecil to speak for her, "because the Chancellor was the Queen's mouth". Cecil, with due gravity, replied that "he was Chancellor of the University, not hers". The Bishop of Ely pleaded that "three words of her mouth were enough". After this little play had been performed, the Queen pronounced a carefully prepared oration which delighted the hearers by its aptness. She assured them of her love for learning, her appreciation of their loyalty, her gratification of all she had seen. One sorrow alone oppressed her; like Alexander the Great, she mourned that she had predecessors who had done so much. She solaced herself by the reflection that Rome was not built in a day, and that she was still young. "My age is not so far advanced but that, before I pay my last debt to nature, if cruel Atropos do not too soon cut the thread of my life, I may erect some noble work." When the applause was over she asked that "all who had heard her speak might drink of the waters of Lethe".

It is on such occasions as these that we see the secret of Elizabeth's charm—her dignity, her ready sympathy, her dexterity, her sprightliness, her social readiness, and her intellectual powers. But even in Cambridge she promised what she did not perform. No noble work was erected by her bounty, and Elizabeth's successors had nothing to fear from her rivalry with those who had gone before. The Duke of Norfolk alone was moved to make a benefaction to Magdalene College.

It was not long before Elizabeth held high state and indulged her love for ceremonial in a matter which seriously concerned her. On September 29 Lord Robert Dudley was created Earl of Leicester so as to fit him for his proposed marriage to Mary of Scotland. We have a description of this scene from the pen of Sir James Melville, who came as Mary's envoy to discuss her future. Melville, on his arrival, found Elizabeth angry at a "despiteful letter" which she had received from Mary. "I was minded," she said, "to answer it with another as despiteful." She took her answer from her pocket and read it; Melville persuaded her to forbear sending it. She asked for Mary's answer to her proposal that she should marry Dudley. Melville answered that it would be discussed at a meeting of commissioners from both realms, in which Mary expected that England would be represented by the Earl of Bedford and Lord Robert Dudley. "You make small account of Lord Robert," said Elizabeth, "seeing you name the Earl of Bedford before him. But I will make him a greater Earl, and you shall see it done before you go home." She called Dudley "her brother and best friend, whom she would have married herself had she minded to take a husband". Being determined to die a virgin, she wished Mary to marry him; this would "free her mind of all fears and suspicions to be offended by any usurpation before her death; being assured that he was so loving and trusty that he would never suffer any such thing to be attempted in her time". So Dudley, with much pomp, was created Baron Denbigh, and afterwards Earl of Leicester. Elizabeth put the mantle on him and girt him with his sword, as he knelt before her; "but she could not refrain from putting her hand in his neck, smilingly tickling him". Then she turned and asked Melville how he liked him. Melville diplomatically answered that the Princess was happy who could reward such a worthy servant. Swiftly Elizabeth pointed to Darnley, who bore the sword of state, and whispered: "Yet you like better of yonder long lad".

Melville gives an account of many interviews with Elizabeth which contain curious details. One day she took him into her bedroom, and opened a little cabinet containing several pictures, each wrapped in paper, with the name written upon it. She took up one labelled "My Lord's picture". Melville pressed to see it, and she reluctantly gave him permission. It was a portrait of Leicester. Melville asked to carry it back for Mary. "No," said Elizabeth, "it is the only one I have." "Your Majesty," answered Melville, "hath the original," and he pointed to Leicester, in the other end of the room. Elizabeth turned to Mary's picture and kissed it with every show of affection. She showed Melville her jewels, and said that if Mary would only follow her counsel she would, in time, have all her possessions. At other times Elizabeth talked with Melville, who had travelled far, about other countries, especially the fashions of ladies' dress. Every day she wore a different costume, and inquired of Melville, as a man of taste, which became her best. "I answered, in my judgment, the Italian dress; which answer, I found, pleased her well, for she delighted to show her golden-coloured hair, wearing a caul and bonnet, as they do in Italy. Her hair was rather reddish than yellow, and curled naturally." She asked Melville which was most beautiful, she or Mary. It needed all his courtliness to escape at last with the answer "that they were both the fairest ladies in their countries". She asked which was tallest. Melville answered Mary. "Then," said she, "she is too high, for I myself am neither too high nor too low." She inquired if Mary played well. Melville, driven to bay, said: "reasonably for a Queen". That evening, after dinner, Elizabeth contrived that Melville should surprise her playing on the virginals, which he admits that she did exceedingly well. On discovering his presence, she rose, "and came forward, seeming to strike him with her hand; alleging that she used not to play before men, but when she was solitary to shun melancholy". However, she asked whether Mary or she played best, and Melville, "in this was obliged to give her the praise". When Melville wished to depart he was stayed two days that he might have an opportunity of seeing the Queen dance. Then she inquired if she or Mary danced best. He answered that Mary "danced not so high nor so disposedly as she did". Elizabeth expressed her longing to see Mary quietly, and Melville sardonically proposed that she should accompany him to Scotland, disguised as a page. She answered with a sigh: "Alas, if I might do it thus!"

It is impossible to say what Elizabeth meant by this conduct; but her want of straightforwardness was infectious. Leicester inquired of Melville what the Queen of Scots thought of him, and was answered coldly. He excused himself for his presumption in seeking Mary's hand and said that the proposal came from Cecil, his secret enemy, "for if I should have appeared desirous of that marriage I should have offended both the Queens and lost their favour". Indeed, in making this confession, Leicester spoke out the true feeling which lay at the bottom of many minds. It was uncertain which Queen's favour was most worth seeking, which of the two would ultimately enjoy the English throne. Cecil was one of the few who were resolutely committed to Elizabeth.

Elizabeth's own wishes about Mary's marriage are obscure. She knew that "the long lad," Darnley, was a candidate; she knew that Leicester was in many ways objectionable. Yet she could not allow her commissioners to name other English nobles, such as Norfolk or Arundel. "She could see none for her own contentation meeter for the purpose than one who for his good gifts she esteemed fit to be placed in the number of kings and princes." She would not even promise to recognize Mary as her successor till the marriage with Leicester had actually been accomplished. But while thus seeming to press Leicester to the exclusion of all others, she allowed Darnley to join his father Lennox, in Scotland, though she knew the projects formed about him. It would almost seem that Elizabeth really wished Mary to contract this marriage. Her alliance with Spain or Austria would have led to a crusade against England. To avert this possibility, to gain time, and to seem willing to do something, Elizabeth proposed the marriage with Leicester. Knowing that this proposal was offensive to Mary, and not wishing it to succeed, she put Darnley in Mary's way, as the least dangerous of possible candidates. At any rate, if Mary married Darnley, her recognition as heir to the

Crown would be deferred for a time; and no one could say what the future might bring forth.

While the matter still hung in the balance, there was no diminution in Elizabeth's familiarity with Leicester. One day he was playing tennis with the Duke of Norfolk, while the Queen was looking on; Leicester took the Queen's handkerchief from her hand to wipe his face, whereon Norfolk's anger against the upstart favourite blazed forth and he threatened to beat him with his racket. Hard words were exchanged on both sides, and the Queen "was sore offended with the Duke". It was obvious that the record of such like scenes should reach Mary's ears and strengthen her objection of marriage with the Queen of England's minion.

When, however, the probability of Mary's marriage with Darnley was discussed in England, its dangers became suddenly apparent. It increased Mary's title and made her seem less of an alien. If it reduced the chances of an invasion of England, it gave greater chance of raising up a faction within the realm itself. Bluster and menace were used to bend Mary's resolution; Lennox and Darnley were recalled to England, but refused to obey. Elizabeth found that she had miscalculated in supposing that the prospect of Mary's marriage with Darnley would cause a disturbance in Scotland. There was no sign of a rising to prevent it. The general feeling of England was somewhat in favour of it: if Elizabeth herself would not marry, it was well that Mary should take a husband of such lineage that her offspring would be nearer of blood to the Tudor line and so more English. In spite of all that Elizabeth could say or do, the marriage was solemnised on July 29, 1565.

Hitherto the two Queens had been watching one another with ill-disguised animosity and suspicion. Now Mary had taken the first step in aggression. Elizabeth would not marry because she could find no match which would strengthen her position, while Mary had secured a husband which brought her nearer to the English Crown. Elizabeth could only retort by reviving the old proposal of marriage with the Austrian Archduke. At least that was something which might be kept continually in reserve. To add to her difficulties, just at this time, the third daughter of the Duke of Suffolk, the only one who remained in the line of succession laid down by Henry VIII., Lady Mary Grey, was found to have contracted a secret marriage. The object of her affections was Thomas Keys, the Queen's serjeant porter. The matter was ludicrous, as the Lady Mary was so small that she was almost a dwarf, while Keys had been chosen for his post owing to his huge proportions. Moreover, the bridegroom was twice the age of the bride and was a widower with several children. Elizabeth committed Keys to the Fleet and Lady Mary to confinement in the houses of friends. The luckless pair were never allowed to meet again. But the last chance of putting forth the successor through the Greys had now disappeared. Mary Stuart stood fronting Elizabeth, dreaded yet inevitable, as her only possible successor, and therefore the necessary representative of all who were discontented in England. If Elizabeth distrusted Mary when she refused to ratify the Treaty of Edinburgh, she now regarded her with dread. In the duel between the two Queens, Mary had made the first hit; and Elizabeth could only gird herself to greater watchfulness in the future. Mary's success was chiefly due to her own imprudence.

NOTE TO PAGE 35: It would seem likely from the researches of Dom Norbert Birt published in *The Elizabethan Religious Settlement*, that a far larger number refused the oath of supremacy. Dom Birt puts the number at 2000, but other students are not prepared to grant that it can have reached that number.—L. C. 1908.

III

ELIZABETH AND
MARY STUART

◄§ The result of Mary's marriage was that, for a time, Elizabeth was reduced to the position of a discredited and somewhat fearful spectator of her doings. At first she had some hopes from a rising of the Protestant nobles under Murray; but she was afraid to help them openly; they were promptly defeated and took refuge in England. Never did Elizabeth sink to a lower depth of duplicity than when Murray, contrary to her wishes, made his way into her presence. She rebuked him for rebellion; she declared that the "Queen of Scots had been her good sister, and such she always expected to find her"; she disclaimed any knowledge of his projects; she dismissed him in disgrace. Having performed this comedy for the good of the ambassadors of France and Spain, she wrote an account of it to Mary. Her only object seemed to be to avoid giving Spain any ground for interference. Absolute caution, however degrading, was, in her opinion, necessary. When she pleaded with Mary in Murray's behalf, her ambassador Randolph was ordered to leave Scotland. Mary's power was daily increasing, and Elizabeth felt herself in serious danger.

From this she was released by the quarrel between Mary and her husband, which led to the murder of Rizzio, at Holyrood, on March 9, 1566. For a time Mary's power seemed broken, but she recovered herself by dauntless energy, and Elizabeth again refused to identify herself with the Scottish rebels. On June 19 was born Mary's son, James, and the news was a bitter blow to Elizabeth. Dropping into a seat, she wailed: "The Queen of Scots is mother of a fair son, and I am but a barren stock". England rejoiced at the news, and Elizabeth felt that it was hard for her to delay much longer the recognition of Mary as her successor. She could not refuse to meet her Parliament, which was sure to raise the question. Her popularity was waning, her enemies were increasing; in many counties preparations were being made for a rising in Mary's behalf.

To escape the despondency caused by these cares, Elizabeth, in August, set forth to visit Oxford, as she had visited Cambridge two years before. First she went to Woodstock and revived the memories of her imprisonment, when peril was as near as it was at present. Leicester, as Chancellor of Oxford, had the advantage of Cecil's experience in making arrangements at Cambridge, and found his task an easy one. There was the same ceremonious reception when she entered the town; but she looked askance at the Vice-Chancellor, Lawrence Humphreys, a noted Puritan, and said: "Mr. Doctor, that loose gown becomes you mighty well; I wonder your notions should be so narrow". She passed between the rows of applauding students to Carfax, in the centre of the town, where the Greek professor greeted her with a Greek oration, to which she made a suitable reply in the same tongue. Thence she went to Christ Church, where she was to lodge. Five days were spent in listening to disputations, visiting the Colleges, and receiving a vast supply of complimentary poems, and attending performances of Latin and English dramas which were acted by the students. A play which told the story of Palamon and Arcite was so lengthy that it occupied two nights; every one opined that its plot was better than that of Damon and Pythias, which was then fashionable. The exercises of dialecticians were listened to with all the admiration and enthusiasm that now has been transferred to athletic sports, and the prowess of disputants was valued as we now value that of a cricketer.

When these contests were over Elizabeth addressed the University in Latin. The evening shadows were falling, and she dexterously began by saying: "Those who do ill hate the light; and because I know that I will speak ill to you, I think this time of gathering darkness is most suitable". She divided what she had to say in two parts: praise and blame. The praise was for the University, the blame for herself. "My parents took good care that I should be well educated, and I had great practice in many languages, of which I take to myself some knowledge; but, though I say this with truth, I say it with modesty. I had many learned teachers, but they laboured in a barren and unproductive field, which brought forth fruit unworthy alike of their toil and of your expectation. Therefore you have praised me abundantly, I am conscious that I deserve not your praise. But I will end this speech, which is full of barbarisms, with one earnest wish and prayer. My prayer is this, that during my lifetime you may be most flourishing, after my death most happy." When she left Oxford the civic magistrates accompanied her to Magdalen Bridge, where their jurisdiction ended; the representatives of the University went to Shotover Hill, where the bounds of the University were reached. There was one last Latin speech; then Elizabeth waved her hand and said: "Farewell, famous University; farewell, my faithful subjects; farewell, dear scholars; and may God bless your studies. Farewell, farewell." Then she rode onwards.

On her return to London Parliament met at the end of September. The question of the succession was uppermost in every mind, and all other business was of secondary importance. In vain Elizabeth tried to avert its discussion by vague promises of marriage and by personal remonstrance with the chief peers. A joint address of the two Houses was presented on November 5, and received an angry answer; what had she done that they should accuse her of "careless care of this her dear realm"? Cecil conveyed the royal displeasure to the Houses and ordered them to be silent on this subject. There was a long discussion if such an order were not against the privileges of the House, but Elizabeth sent for the Speaker and repeated her command "that there should be no further argument". A member strayed into the forbidden subject, and Elizabeth had him put under arrest. The Commons began to consider their privileges. Elizabeth saw that she had gone too far.

She released the imprisoned member, and sending for the Speaker, informed him that "she did revoke her two former commandments requiring the House no further at this time to proceed in the matter". But she nursed her wrath till the end of the session, when she dismissed Parliament, saying at the end of her speech:—

"Do you think that either I am so unmindful of your surety by succession, wherein is all my care, considering I know myself to be but mortal? No, I warrant you. Or that I went about to break your liberties? No, it never was my meaning; but to stay you before you fell into the ditch. For all things have their time; and although perhaps you may have after me a better, learneder, or wiser, yet I assure you, none more careful over you. And therefore henceforth, whether I live to see the like assembly or no, or whoever it be, yet beware how you prove your Prince's patience as you have now done mine.

"And now to conclude all this. Notwithstanding, not meaning to make a Lent of Christmas, the most part of you may assure yourselves that you depart in your Prince's grace."

Elizabeth had no doubt of her power to rule and was determined that no one should doubt her capacity to do so. There were matters which she alone could manage, and she demanded implicit trust in her discretion where questions of national policy were concerned. Her objections to the discussion of her marriage and of the succession were not founded on personal grounds. She claimed that she alone could judge what was for the real interests of her realm.

Events in Scotland came to her help and occupied the minds of men. On February 10, 1567, Darnley was murdered, and Elizabeth received the news with every appearance of sorrow. It must, however, have given her a sense of profound relief. She had felt that Mary was gaining and that herself was losing. Now was an opportunity of asserting her superiority. Her own desire all along had been to maintain Mary in Scotland, but to reduce her to a position of dependence on herself. Hitherto she had been baffled:

now she might succeed. So she adopted the attitude of Mary's candid friend and adviser. She wrote to her expressing her horror at the news of the murder; and then continued: "Madam, I should ill fulfil the part either of a faithful cousin or of an affectionate friend, if I were to content myself with saying pleasant things to you and made no effort to preserve your honour. I cannot but tell you what all the world is thinking. Men say that, instead of seizing the murderers, you are looking through your fingers while they escape. For myself I beseech you to believe that I would not harbour such a thought for all the wealth of the world. I entreat you to let no interest, no persuasion, keep you from proving to every one that you are a noble Princess and a loyal wife." With this letter was a proposal for the ratification of the Treaty of Edinburgh, and the establishment of a Church in Scotland on the lines of the Church of England. With good advice went a request for substantial advantages.

Whether or no Mary would have followed Elizabeth's advice is an open question. It is certain that she did not; and her marriage with Bothwell, on May 15, was the signal for a rising against her. She was taken prisoner and was confined in Lochleven Castle on June 17. Elizabeth gave no help to the confederate Lords and entirely disapproved of their action. She was sensitive about the rights of Princes. She felt that she owed much to the forbearance of foreign Powers, and was resolved to set a good example. At the same time, she purposed to use the position of self-appointed mediator in a lofty manner. She sent her commands to the Scottish nobles as one having authority. They were ordered to release the Queen, to inquire into Bothwell's guilt for Darnley's murder, to provide for a meeting of the Scottish Parliament and a general pacification, and to bring Prince James to England for safe keeping. Elizabeth certainly asked enough and asserted unmistakably the claims of a feudal superiority. Her ministers saw that her demands were hopeless of attainment; but, in matters which concerned her position as a Sovereign, Elizabeth would brook no advice. She preferred the issues of bold diplomacy to action. The duties of one Sovereign Prince towards another were to be determined by the Sovereign alone.

Perhaps Elizabeth was saving her personal credit at small cost. She knew that her demands were impossible. A full investigation of recent occurrences in Scotland was not to be thought of, as every one of position was involved either in the murder of Rizzio or of Darnley; and an inquiry once instituted could not be limited. The Lords refused to listen to Elizabeth's envoy, Sir Nicholas Throgmorton. Elizabeth wrote to him: "We do detest the murder of our cousin the King; but the head cannot be subject to the foot, and we cannot recognize in them any right to call their Sovereign to account. You shall plainly tell them that, if they determine anything to the deprivation of the Queen, their Sovereign, we are well assured of our determination that we will make ourselves a plain party against them to the revenge of their Sovereign for all posterity." The Lords extracted from Mary her signature to a document in which she abdicated in favour of her son. Throgmorton publicly protested, and privately pleaded that, at least, Mary's life should be spared. Elizabeth threatened war, and Cecil pointed out that "the malice of the world would say that she had used severity to the Lords to urge them to rid away the Queen". Elizabeth had failed in her plan of keeping Mary on the Scottish throne, weak, discredited and dependent on herself, who had established her position as arbiter of Scottish affairs, and would organise the country on the model of England.

All this, however, added to the perplexity of those who were anxious about England's future. Mary of Scotland had been tacitly regarded as Elizabeth's successor. Now all was plunged in uncertainty. Troubles in the Netherlands had led Philip of Spain to send a large army to subdue the rebels; if it succeeded, England lay temptingly near. Elizabeth's marriage could alone avert danger, and the claims of the Archduke Charles of Austria were again pressed upon her by the Council. Though a Romanist, he had learned to tolerate Lutheranism, and so would not be hostile to the English Church. By Elizabeth's marriage with him England would be on friendly terms with Spain and would be recognised as allied with the Courts of Europe.

So the Earl of Sussex was sent to Vienna to see if matters could be arranged. The chief point concerned religion. Sussex was to point out that uniformity was a principle of English politics: "Many inconveniences had happened in other countries from maintaining contrariety in religion. England differed from all other States that it could not suffer those diversities of religion which others were seen to do. The law touched no man's conscience, so as public order was not violated by external act or teaching." The Queen could not change her laws for a marriage. Charles was invited to return with Sussex and see for himself. Sussex reported that Charles was willing to come to England and would accept all the Queen's conditions, save on the matter of his religion. He would accompany the Queen to public service; he asked only for the use of a private chapel where he could hear Mass, which no Englishman should be allowed to attend. These were reasonable requests, which Elizabeth might have granted if she had been in earnest. But Elizabeth was never in earnest about her marriage, and she knew that if Charles once came to England it would be difficult to find an escape. If he had consented to abandon his religious opinions, that would have been a sacrifice which would have satisfied her vanity and would have bound him to herself. As it was, she doubted if a Romanist Prince in England might not cause trouble. "God," she said, "had so far prospered her by keeping England in peace, while France, Scotland and Flanders were torn by war; she minded still to please Him by continuing her whole realm in one manner of religion." Yet, if the Archduke would come, all might be settled; during his visit he should have "such use of his religion as should be found possible". If he came in the hopes of procuring toleration for the Romanists, "his coming would be both vain and dishonourable".

After such an equivocal answer, nothing was to be done. Charles refused to put himself in a false position, and Elizabeth would give him no positive assurance. She was not entirely insincere in her advances; but she was not satisfied that the advantages to be gained were equivalent to the risk which would be incurred. Her ministers looked only to the present; Elizabeth looked to the future. She had been accustomed all her life to live amid uncertainties, and had none of the faith which makes a bold venture. The return must be quite sure before she would make a sacrifice. She would pursue a project up to the final point and then reject it. She wondered that others did not see difficulties as clearly as herself; but she could not follow their superior confidence. Sorely to the disappointment of Cecil, the negotiation with Charles came to an end and was not renewed.

On May 2, 1568, Mary of Scotland escaped from Lochleven Castle and was again at the head of a band of adherents. Elizabeth's position was again very difficult. She had defended Mary when she was a prisoner, what was she to do now she was at large? Elizabeth's real wish was to set Mary again on the throne, but in such a way as to make her, and through her Scotland, dependent on England. Hence when Mary was in prison, Elizabeth was her friend; now that Mary was striving to win back her position by herself, Elizabeth remembered her misdeeds. She wrote Mary a letter in which she reminded her that in the past she had "shown small respect for her state and honour"; she was prepared to help her if she would now follow her advice, which was to desist from force and submit to Elizabeth's arbitration between herself and her subjects. But before Elizabeth's message reached her, Mary's troops were scattered at Langside and she was a fugitive in Galloway.

There were three courses possible for Mary: to remain in hiding till her adherents had again rallied; to sail for France; or to take refuge in England. In the light of after events, it seems strange that she chose the last of these possibilities. But it suited her temperament to play an adventurous game, and she thought that by a little pressure she could force Elizabeth to intervene on her behalf. On May 16 she crossed the Solway, and was escorted to the Castle of Carlisle. Such had been Mary's haste that she had brought with her no change of dress; and it is odd to find that Carlisle could not supply her needs. When Elizabeth heard of her condition she sent her some clothing. When the parcel was opened, it contained "two torn shifts, two pieces of black velvet, two pair of shoes, and nothing else". Sir Francis Knowles, who brought this munificent gift, was driven by shame to say "that Her Highness's maid had mistaken and sent such things necessary for such a maid-servant as she was herself". Was it insolence, or parsimony, or carelessness, which led to such an extraordinary breach of courtesy? Whichever it might be, it betokened ill for Elizabeth's hospitality.

Mary demanded that she should be received at Court and should be allowed to explain her position to Elizabeth. This demand raised great difficulties. Mary claimed to be the second person in the realm, and her reception at Court would have been a recognition of her claim. She was informed that she must prove her innocence of the charges laid against her before she could be admitted to the Queen's presence. She then demanded "to be allowed to pass into France to seek aid at other Princes' hands". This was hard to refuse on any personal ground; but it was too much to expect that Elizabeth would run the risk of provoking French interference in Scotland. The only answer she could give was that "all convenient means would be used for Mary's relief and comfort". In fact, Elizabeth still clung to her old policy. Mary, weak and discredited, was to be restored to nominal rule in Scotland, while really reduced to dependence on England. So Elizabeth assured her that she would "have care both of her life and honour". "Does it seem strange," she went on, "that you are not allowed to see me? I entreat you to put yourself in my place. When you are acquitted of this crime I will receive you with all honour; till that is done, I may not." Later, she explained that she must not receive her, or else she would seem to be partial, and "the other side would not accept her arbitration, so that she would be unable to help her". Elizabeth gradually slipped into the position of judge, in spite of Mary's remonstrances; but she was going to do the best she could for Mary. Her intention was to have enough evidence produced to slightly justify the Lords and slightly inculpate Mary: then she would suggest a genial compromise, which would require her constant intervention to maintain.

It was a difficult game to play, because both parties were to be deluded into putting themselves into Elizabeth's hands, on the supposition that she would favour them. As for a judicial inquiry into the circumstances of Darnley's murder, that was impossible in itself; and certainly no impartial tribunal could be constructed to try the case. Elizabeth put forward the inquiry as a necessary preliminary for her action, but neither party would agree to the inquiry till they knew what that action would be. So Elizabeth led Mary to suppose that she intended to restore her in Scotland, whatever happened, while she informed Murray that she did not mean to restore her if she were found guilty of the murder. She thus rendered it tolerably certain that evidence of Mary's guilt would be produced. Then she nominated three Commissioners who were to meet the representatives of Mary and of the Scottish Lords at York. The Commissioners were fairly chosen to represent different opinions in England. They were the Duke of Norfolk, the leader of the old nobility; the Earl of Sussex, a statesman of the old school; and Sir Ralph Sadler, a capable official of the new type which had arisen under Henry VIII. When the Commissioners met at York, in October, Murray showed them privately some letters, purporting to have been discovered in a casket belonging to Mary, which incriminated her of devising with Bothwell the murder of Darnley. What was intended to be a political compromise threatened to become a criminal trial, and Elizabeth had to consider what she would do. She dissolved the conference at York and summoned it to Westminster. She laid the evidence against Mary before a Council of the Peers. She added five, amongst them Leicester, Cecil and Bacon, to the number of the English Commissioners, who began a kind of private inquiry into Mary's guilt. When Mary protested against this jurisdiction, Murray was set up as the criminal and was required to prove his charge. The evidence was placed before a number of the English peers, who were of opinion that until some answer had been made, Elizabeth could not admit Mary to her presence. It is clear that Elizabeth hoped by thus gradually tightening the coils of the net round Mary to induce her to admit her guilt, confirm her abdication, and allow James to be educated in England as successor to the English Crown. But Mary refused and Elizabeth was afraid to push matters to extremities. She stopped short and left everything to the chance of the future. Murray was told that "nothing had been brought against the Lords which impaired their honour and allegiance"; but also that nothing "had been sufficiently produced against the Queen, their Sovereign, whereby the Queen of England should take evil opinion of the Queen, her good sister". With this impotent conclusion the Conference ended.

Elizabeth had failed in arranging matters, as she hoped, by an advantageous compromise on political grounds. Anything of the nature of a trial was out of the question; but, short of this, Mary's reputation had been damaged as far as it could be. For the present, she would remain in captivity in England, till some opportunity offered for sagacious action to which she might lend her name. Elizabeth had, by this time, contracted the habit of putting off unpleasant business and leaving it undone. She had put off her own marriage and the settlement of the succession; the disposal of Mary of Scotland might conveniently be added to the list, as being cognate to them. Elizabeth was so accustomed to live from hand to mouth that her policy consisted in delay. She was willing to decide if the opportunity was favourable; but the opportunity rarely offered all that she wanted. So she waited for a convenient season. If she had not restored Mary, at least she had not betrayed her. She had done enough to obtain general acquiescence to the important point that Mary ought not to be received at Court. Doubtless, on this point, she recalled her own personal experiences in her young days. Perhaps she felt a certain pleasure in facing the claim on her own dexterity, and was of opinion that she could manage Mary Stuart more skilfully than Mary Tudor had managed herself. She felt a perverse satisfaction in watching how things would turn out.

There were, however, other dangers threatening Elizabeth. The Spanish troops of Alva were victorious in the Netherlands; and Elizabeth could not flatter herself that Philip was her friend. She had tried his patience in many ways, as she discovered that he could not interfere in English affairs through fear that Mary Stuart would be a firm ally of France. Now that Mary's fortunes had waned, she would be a puppet in the hands of any one who acted as her deliverer. Philip had suffered much from England. It was of primary importance to him to have safe communication by sea between Spain and the Netherlands; and England, though at peace with him, was a constant source of annoyance at sea.

During the last few years there had been a wonderful development of piracy, in which the energies of Englishmen found an outlet. England was passing through a social change in which agricultural pursuits were sinking in importance before industry and commerce. There was a displacement of population which opened out the way to adventure, and piracy become a profitable trade. The government naturally wished for the growth of English seamanship and the command of the narrow seas. It winked at piracy as a temporary matter, till some better mode of training seamen could be found. England could not afford a navy; its fisheries were decaying, its carrying trade was not large. Good management might increase the occupation for Englishmen at sea; meanwhile they must find their own occupation and they found it in piracy. Elizabeth was not sorry if Spain was the sufferer; she only wished to keep things within the limits of decency. This, however, was difficult, and complaints were many. At last, in 1564, Philip determined to give Elizabeth a lesson. Taking advantage of her war with France, he arrested all the English fleets in Spanish harbours and excluded English traders from the Flemish ports. This drove Elizabeth to apologise and to promise to do her utmost to suppress pirates. She ordered Sir Peter Carew to clear the seas between Devonshire and Ireland; but he was to do it at his own expense and pay himself out of the booty which he could capture. This was not a profitable undertaking and little was done. A Commission met at Bruges to settle differences between England and Spain; but the English commissioners had nothing to urge in their defence. "Our men," they wrote, "in their offences are so far out of all order, and the cases are so lamentable, if the accounts be true, that we scant tell how to open our mouths for any reasonable satisfaction therein."

Nor was it only in the Channel that Spain had to complain of English depredation. In the Spanish possessions in America it had been found that the native Indians were unsuited for labour in the mines, and negroes were brought from Africa to work in their stead. This traffic, however, was carefully regulated and was carried on under a licence from the Spanish Government. John Hawkins, however, discovered that a good business was to be done in smuggling negroes into the Spanish colonies contrary to the law. On his first voyage, half of his return cargo was seized and confiscated at Cadiz, and Elizabeth was admonished to prevent this illicit trading. However, Hawkins had learned wisdom by experience and was not discouraged. In his second venture, Leicester, Pembroke, and even the Queen herself, are said to have taken shares. Hawkins sailed with his negroes to several Spanish ports and sold them in defiance of the Governor. He paid those who had taken shares in his undertaking 60 per cent., and was openly received at Court. In 1567 Hawkins sailed again, but this time his good fortune deserted him. As he lay in the harbour of San Juan de Ulloa a Spanish fleet arrived and captured his ships, leaving him to escape with two small tenders, which made their way with difficulty to Plymouth Harbour in December, 1568.

Now it chanced that, just at this time, there lay in the harbour ships laden with money for the Duke of Alva. Philip had borrowed from Genoese bankers and the dollars were divided, for greater safety, among several vessels, which were trying to escape the dangers of the Channel. Some of them had thought it prudent to take refuge in English harbours, so as to elude the pirates, and lay there in some anxiety, waiting a favourable opportunity to slip out unperceived. Hawkins, smarting under his disaster, thirsted for revenge. He told his story in his own way: as Philip had robbed English subjects, the Queen might seize Philip's ships till recompense was made. The suggestion fitted in with political expediency. Elizabeth was not prepared to help the Netherlanders in their revolt, but she was glad to check Alva's progress. He was anxiously waiting for money, and the loss of it would cripple him. So the ships were seized and the money was brought to London. Don Guerau d'Espes, the Spanish ambassador, sought an explanation from the Queen, but it was a week before he could obtain an interview. Then Elizabeth told him that as she had need of a loan, she had found that the Genoese, to whom the money belonged, were willing to lend it to her instead of Philip. In vain the ambassador protested. She answered that the owners might lend where they chose; if they preferred her security to that of Philip, no one could complain.

To this outrageous conduct Alva replied by arresting all English residents in the Netherlands. Elizabeth retaliated by arresting the Flemings and Spaniards in England. It is true that England had the advantage in these reprisals; but the interruption of trade caused discontent, and the prospect of war with Spain was serious. Elizabeth had to quiet matters by issuing a proclamation which tried to throw the blame on Spain. The money, she said, was the property of some merchants: its safe custody had been forced upon her; she was considering if she might not borrow part of it, when Alva, without asking an explanation, laid violent hands on English ships and cargoes in the Netherlands, and had forced her to retaliate. However, Elizabeth and her Council were ashamed of their dishonest proceeding, and winced before the jests of the Spanish ambassador. He was confined to his house, and his correspondence was read. In a letter to a friend, he wrote:

"Do not be surprised to hear that I am arrested. In this island there are all the enchantments of Amadis, and I am a prisoner of Queen Oriana." Cecil's soul burned with wrath. The letter still remains with his endorsement: "Against the Queen's Majesty Oriana". Don Guerau was told that "such vain fancies taken from Amadis of Gaul were unworthy of a person holding his office. He would be treated as a seditious, insolent person, unworthy to be admitted into the presence of a Prince." Don Guerau had the best of it, for he answered by expressing his surprise that the Council should have opened letters not addressed to them, and should have failed to understand their contents. He politely offered to send them a man "to whom the Spanish tongue is natural" that he might interpret his harmless jests. Cecil was placed at a disadvantage and nourished a grudge.

It was, however, inevitable that this prospect of a Spanish war, joined to the excitement caused by the presence of Mary, should awaken great anxieties and should bring to light hidden sources of discontent. Elizabeth's attitude towards Spain was due to Cecil's advice. The old nobles looked on Cecil as an upstart, were jealous of his influence with the Queen and regarded his policy as hazardous. Hitherto Elizabeth had tried a cautious compromise; she had aimed above all things at keeping the country together; she had been more anxious not to commit herself to anything that could cause discontent than to assume a definite position. It was natural for her advisers to wish for certainty: it was equally natural for Elizabeth to find her safety in cautious ambiguity, which she concealed under occasional outbursts of self-will in personal matters. But there must come a time when compromise must be tested, and differing opinions surge against the barriers erected to keep them down.

The result of the conference about Mary had shown that Elizabeth would not recognise her succession. Yet there was no one else, and some arrangement must be made. Already, during the conference, a plan had been formed for Mary's marriage with the Duke of Norfolk, and this plan had the sympathy of a large party of the English nobles. By the side of this was a plan for the overthrow of Cecil, which was cordially supported by Leicester. We have an account of an incident which shows how things stood in the middle of February, 1569. The Queen was talking with Leicester and Cecil, at one end of the room, when Norfolk and several others were present. Elizabeth supported Cecil's opinion against Leicester, who angrily exclaimed that her throne would never be safe till Cecil's head was off his shoulders. She raised her voice in passion and threatened to send Leicester to the Tower. Norfolk remarked to those standing with him that Leicester was in favour so long as he echoed Cecil, but was in danger if he had an opinion of his own. "But, by God," he added, "this shall not be; some remedy must be found for this." "Pray God, it may be so," said Lord Northampton, "I have ever wished it." Then Norfolk advanced to the Queen and said that when her anger was past, and she could reflect quietly on the state of the country, she would see the need of wiser counsel; he and his friends would consider what ought to be done. Elizabeth swept out of the room in mingled wrath and dismay.

To understand what followed, some account of the Duke of Norfolk's position is necessary. Thomas Howard was the son of the poet Earl of Surrey, who was beheaded by Henry VIII., and sprang of a house which had long claimed the chief place in England. He had added to his importance by a series of rich marriages. His first wife was the daughter of the Earl of Arundel, and his son by that marriage was heir to the Arundel domains. His second wife was similarly heiress of Lord Audley of Walden. His third wife was the widow of Lord Dacre of Gilsland, next to the Percies the most powerful of the nobles on the English Border. On her death, in 1567, Norfolk was again a widower, at the age of thirty-one. It is no wonder that, after reaping such rich harvests from matrimony, it seemed to him that a kingdom was the only remaining dower which had not fallen to his lot. The suggestion that he should marry Mary came originally from the Scottish side, during the conference at York. Later, he had an interview with Murray, who encouraged him to hope that the proposal would be laid before Elizabeth by an envoy from the Scottish Parliament. The general uncertainty in England and the desire to reverse Cecil's policy towards Spain drove many of the chief nobles to acquiesce in the plan as the wisest and safest course to pursue.

But there was one point in which Norfolk was weak, and Cecil soon discovered it. Norfolk was in debt, and could not afford to forego any personal advantage. After the death of his last wife he obtained the wardship of her children by Lord Dacre. The only boy died in May, 1569; and Norfolk determined to marry the three daughters to his three sons, and so secure for his family the Dacre estates. Their title, however, was disputed by the last owner's brother, Leonard Dacre, who claimed as heir male, and was recognised as such in his neighbourhood. When Cecil discovered the conspiracy against himself he offered Norfolk and Arundel full powers to go to Spain and settle the dispute with Philip; but, at the same time, he offered Norfolk his influence to have the lawsuit about the Dacre inheritance settled in his favour. Norfolk accepted the offer, and a legal decision was given against Leonard Dacre on July 19. This had the effect of separating Norfolk from the northern Lords, who all sided with their neighbour Dacre. They were, moreover, strong adherents of the Pope, and preferred a husband for Mary who would be decidedly on the Papal side. Hence parties were again divided. Norfolk fell back on Cecil and trusted to gain Elizabeth's consent to his marriage with Mary. The northern Lords plotted to carry off Mary and allow her to marry whomsoever the King of Spain suggested. Mary communicated with both parties, and was ready to accept whichever was successful.

Norfolk's influence led the Council to vote, on August 27, for the settlement of the succession by the marriage of Mary to some English nobleman; but he had not the courage to plead his own cause with Elizabeth. He proposed that the Council should wait upon her in a body and state their wishes. It is significant of the effect of Elizabeth's personality that they all declined, and Norfolk was too terrified to speak for himself. When he tried to do so "he fell into an ague and was fain to get him to bed without his dinner". Elizabeth was going on progress, and Norfolk followed her, trying to screw up courage to speak. On her side she endeavoured to lead him to the point. One morning, in the garden at Richmond, she called him and asked him what news. Norfolk said he knew of none. "None?" said the Queen. "You come from London and can bring no news of a marriage?" A lady came up with some flowers, and Norfolk slunk away. Leicester pleaded for him; but Norfolk could not speak for himself. The Queen grew weary, and one day, at dinner, "gave him a nip, bidding him to take care of his pillow".

In fact, she was anxiously waiting some assurance of Norfolk's fidelity to herself, and was doubting if she could trust him. She felt some alarm and told Leicester that "if she consented, she would be in the Tower before four months were over". Norfolk was doubting if he should ask the Queen's consent or join the plan to rescue Mary by force. At last he could bear the suspense no longer, and on September 15 hastily left the Court. Elizabeth at once returned to Windsor, and sent the Earl of Huntingdon, whom she could fully trust, to bring Mary to the safe keeping of the strong castle of Tutbury. It was now too late for a rising, and Norfolk could only advise the northern Earls that Mary was too securely guarded to be rescued. Then he wrote to Elizabeth that "he never intended to deal otherwise than he had her favour to do". He withdrew to his house at Kenninghall, and when summoned to London pleaded illness. Leicester sent him a message, that if he continued disobedient he would be proclaimed a traitor. Having no settled policy and unable to face this threat, Norfolk returned to London and was confined to his house. Elizabeth wished to bring him to trial for treason, but Cecil interceded. He had taken the measure of Norfolk's character, and wrote: "Better marry him to somebody. Provide him with a wife and his hopes of the Scottish Queen will pass away." However, on October 8

Norfolk was committed to the Tower, and Elizabeth at first declared that she would have his head off by her own authority if the law could not condemn him.

She was deeply moved by a sense of surrounding danger which she could not clearly discover. Norfolk's conduct had impressed her with a sense of his disloyalty, and he had been supported by many whom she trusted, even by Leicester. Cecil was afraid to prosecute his inquiries too far, for he was anxiously watching the northern counties, where devotion to the old religion and to Mary's cause was strongest. The Earls of Northumberland and Westmoreland were at the head of a body of gentlemen who had been prepared to rise for Mary's rescue. They were furious at Norfolk's cowardice, and were waiting for another opportunity for action. They were carefully watched by the Earl of Sussex, who was President of the Council of the North; and they felt that the inquiries about Norfolk would reveal their complicity. They received a summons to London, but sent thinly-veiled excuses. At last, on November 14, they threw off disguise, entered the city of Durham, took possession of the Cathedral, tore in pieces the English Bible and Prayer-Book, and celebrated Mass. Thence they marched southwards, intending to release Mary from Tutbury; but when they reached Tadcaster they found that Mary had been transferred to Coventry. They paused irresolutely, and as the country did not rise in their favour, withdrew northwards. This gave time for the Queen to gather forces; and the rebel army, dismayed at the indecision of its leaders, gradually dispersed. At the end of November Northumberland and Westmoreland fled across the Border, where they found refuge in the trackless dales.

There remained another conspirator, more dangerous because he was more capable. Leonard Dacre had not taken part in the rising, but professed to hold the Castle of Naworth for the Queen. There he gathered arms and provisions, and was at the head of a formidable army of borderers amongst whom his name was held in high repute. Elizabeth ordered Sussex to send him to

London; but Sussex admitted that he was powerless. Luckily the Governor of Berwick, Henry Carey, Lord Hunsdon, was Elizabeth's cousin, being the son of Anne Boleyn's sister. His assured fidelity gave him courage to undertake a perilous enterprise. When Dacre knew himself to be suspected he threw off the mask and summoned the Scottish borderers to his aid. Unless prompt action were taken the rising would break out again, on a larger scale and under a more competent commander. Hunsdon determined to attack Naworth, if possible; if not, to reinforce the garrison of Carlisle. Hastily collecting such forces as he could—they only amounted to 1500 men—he set out from Hexham by night on February 19, 1570. He soon found that he was marching through a hostile country. Beacons blazed on every hill, and everywhere were heard the shouts of horsemen gathering for the fray. When he reached Naworth, at daybreak he found it strongly fortified and impregnable from its position. Dacre was expecting him with 3000 men. Not daring to give battle, he pursued his road to Carlisle. In front of him ran the little river Gelt, difficult to pass owing to its precipitous banks. Dacre pursued him, expecting to catch him in a trap, and charged as he stood hesitating by the cliffs, which cut off his advance. But Hunsdon's men stood firm, and fired with trained precision. The furious charge of the border horsemen was checked, and Hunsdon's cavalry fell upon them in the flank. Dacre lost courage and fled to Liddesdale; his troops, deprived of a leader, rode for their homes.

The battle of the Gelt is little known in military annals; but it deserves to rank high among the battles fought on English soil. Hunsdon was outnumbered two to one; his position was dangerous; and his men were wearied by a long night's march. His defeat would have been disastrous; the victory was due to his courage and skill. Elizabeth thanked him with a warmth that was unusual. "I doubt not, my Harry," she wrote with her own hand, "whether that the victory given me more joyed me, or that you were by God appointed the instrument of my glory. And I assure you that for my country's sake the first might suffice; but, for my heart's contentation, the second more pleased me. It likes me not a little that, with a good testimony of your faith, there is seen a stout courage of your mind, that trusted more to the goodness of your quarrel than to the weakness of your numbers."

Elizabeth had been thoroughly alarmed by this revolt, and, when her fear was over, she clamoured for vengeance. Not only was she incensed that any one should rebel against such an excellent Sovereign, but she sorely grudged the money which she had been compelled to spend in her own defence. Her desire was to strike terror into all, but to combine punishment with economy. Sussex was ordered to seize all who had been concerned in the rebellion. Those who had no land were to be dealt with by martial law; a certain number were to be hanged at once on their village green, as a warning to their neighbours. Those who were possessed of land were to be tried, so that the Crown might have the advantage of the forfeitures which could follow on their conviction for treason. In accordance with these instructions, some 600 or 700 peasants were hanged, whose only crime was that they had followed those whom they regarded as their leaders. The men with possessions were carefully tried and sentenced in such a way that the greatest pecuniary advantage might be obtained. Moreover, Elizabeth was ceaseless in her efforts to secure the Earls of Northumberland and Westmoreland that she might make certain of their attainder.

Elizabeth was not naturally cruel and was generally averse to bloodshed. But, on this occasion, she lost her self-control, and was heedless of the remonstrances of her ministers. Yet never was an occasion when magnanimity would better have befitted a Sovereign. The complete failure of the northern rising showed how firmly Elizabeth was seated on her throne. The crisis, which had been so long dreaded, came and passed harmlessly away. Europe had long supposed that Elizabeth ruled over England only on sufferance; that the great majority of her people were opposed to her actions; that if she was seriously challenged she would fall. The challenge came, and only proved that Elizabeth possessed the affection and confidence of her people. It was hopeless to overthrow her by a rebellion. For that purpose, assassination or foreign invasion alone could avail.

IV

THE EXCOMMUNICATION
OF ELIZABETH

 § Notwithstanding the failure of the rising of the north, it was an indication of the growing danger of Elizabeth's position. There was in England itself a party which was irreconcilably opposed to her rule, and was only waiting for an opportunity to overthrow it. The ground of its opposition was religious, and it called in question the title of Elizabeth as the legitimate holder of the Crown. If she was not the rightful Queen, she had no claim on the loyalty of her subjects; it was their duty to depose her and set Mary Stuart in her stead. These were the ideas which lay behind the rising of the north. It was the conception which animated that revolt which made it dangerous; and the danger remained after the revolt had been put down.

It was obvious from the beginning of Elizabeth's reign that such a party must exist; but the questions to be decided were—how large that party would be, how much vitality it would possess, and what outside help it would obtain. The decision depended on two things—the success of the religious settlement in England, and the fortunes of that other settlement which must soon be made by the Roman Church abroad. At Elizabeth's accession there was doubt on both these points; ten years later the doubt had been removed. Elizabeth was bound to confess that England was not united in religion, while the Church of Rome had removed some of its abuses, had strengthened its organisation, and had gathered round it a devoted body of adherents.

It was, indeed, a difficult thing for England to settle down again into absolute unity in religion. The mass of the people were satisfied with the removal of those pressing and practical abuses which had been connected with the Roman jurisdiction. They welcomed the greater demand on their intelligence, and on their co-operation in public worship, which was made by the simplification of the old services. But the rapid changes under Edward VI. and Mary had necessarily lowered the efficiency of the body of the clergy. Men who live through rapid transitions either become violent partisans, or grow timorous, cynical, or indifferent. The leaders on either side had been ejected in turns; the clergy who remained were not men of strong character or much capacity. Moreover they were a diminishing body, and it was not always easy to replace them. Young men of promise might well hesitate, in the face of prevailing uncertainty, and turn to some other career than that of the priesthood. If the old clergy were indifferent, the younger clergy were often of little learning and of lowly birth. The benefices were mostly poor, and the churches had suffered from excessive zeal in removing monuments of superstition. The services in parish churches were, as a rule, lacking in dignity; and as they were intelligible, their shortcomings were immediately perceptible.

These, however, were temporary difficulties, which would soon have disappeared had the religious zeal of England been united. But the great majority of English theologians had been driven to leave England before the Marian persecution. Partly the natural resentment inspired by their wrongs led them to dislike the religious system in whose interest those wrongs were inflicted; partly they took refuge for greater safety in the regions where the most advanced forms of Protestantism prevailed. The English exiles absorbed much of the theology of Calvin, and when they returned home were anxious to introduce it into England. They had no sympathy with the conception which lay at the root of the changes made in the forms of the English Church —the acceptance of the results of the New Learning, the abolition of all usages which had grown up only through unreasoning sentiment and perverse ingenuity, and the maintenance of all that

had existed in primitive times. They were men of a later generation, who had grown up in times of strife and were interested in
finding weapons which could be wielded with effect, bulwarks
which were strong against assault. The first generation of reformers hopefully removed abuses, and trusted to general intelligence to understand the reasonableness of what was done. Their
successors felt more keenly the force of the old system, which
was interwoven with popular life and sentiment. They wished to
sweep it away altogether, and set up in its stead a new theology, a
new form of Church government and of public worship. They
thought that it must come to this in the long run, in England also;
and they wished to precipitate the decision. The number of the
adherents of Calvin was not large, but it consisted of resolute and
earnest men, who were intent on spreading their opinions. They
had all the power which comes from zeal. They were strong in
the Universities, where young men were affected by what
seemed to them the advanced opinions which must rule the future. Some of the Bishops had strong sympathies with them, at
least so far that they hesitated to silence men, whose Christian
zeal was beyond dispute, in a time when zeal was not too common. Indeed the temper of Englishmen was opposed to any
undue exercise of authority in matters of opinion. Men must be
heard before they were condemned. It might be that after a period of discussion things would settle themselves.

But all this gave an appearance of uncertainty to the system of
the English Church. Many minds, which would have been contented after a while with the Prayer-Book, paused to ask themselves what security they had that it would be maintained. They
thought that they might soon be called upon to choose between
Rome and Geneva, and the attractions of the old system were
more keenly felt at this prospect. The conflict which was raging
on the Continent was introduced into England. The English
Church was strong enough to save the nation as a whole from the
horrors of religious warfare. It represented the religious feeling
of the great majority of the people, and exercised a dominant in-

fluence over the future of England. But it was not permitted to include the entire people. There were formed two parties, one of which looked to Rome, and trusted to recover its superiority by foreign help; the other was determined to capture the English Church, and mould it by persistent energy into the form which it preferred.

So, on the one hand, there were Englishmen who went abroad, that they might move the Pope to excommunicate Elizabeth and declare war against a heretical Queen. On the other hand, there were Englishmen who stayed at home and consulted Calvin how far they could conform to the English Prayer-Book, and what steps they were to take in the direction of further change. Both of these parties were dangerous to the national welfare, which required, above all else, that England should be united and should give no opportunity for intervention in its affairs. But, for practical purposes, the danger lay in the direction of Rome, and it was judged necessary to take measures of defence. In the Parliament of 1562 an Act was passed for the "Assurance of the Queen's Power over all Estates," making all who upheld the Pope's authority or jurisdiction liable to the penalties of præmunire, and requiring the oath of the royal supremacy to be taken by all who held office, lay or spiritual, in the realm. It is true that Archbishop Parker admonished his suffragans to proceed gently in administering the oath, and to overlook the older clergy, who, at least, were silent. But the Puritan clergy soon began a protest against ecclesiastical vestments. They would have neither surplice, hood, nor square cap. Clothes worn by Papists were like meat offered to idols: they were bound to abstain from all appearance of evil. The unfortunate legacy of fighting great principles over outward trifles was bequeathed to the English Church. Yet beneath all this unseemly discord was developing that conception of liberty which has made the English character what it is. Obvious as are its drawbacks for the purposes of orderly arrangement, it fostered a spirit of sincerity and self-respect which lie at the root of national character. The man who insists on thinking for himself, learns to act for himself, and gains a sense of duty and regard for justice, on which the welfare of a community must ultimately depend.

While England was thus engaged in raising questions which it has not yet succeeded in solving, Rome was engaged in casting overboard what could no longer be carried, and in forging its unwieldy system into compact strength for the purpose of aggression. The Council of Trent marks the dividing line between the mediæval Church and modern Romanism. It collected scattered forces, revived ancient claims, and prepared to reconquer the realms that had been lost. In so doing, the Roman Church largely assimilated the spirit of the Spanish monarchy, and went forth with the one desire of putting down heresy by the sword and the stake. Hitherto the Papal attitude towards England had been uncertain. Now there was no longer room for doubt. It was a rebellious province which must be forcibly brought back to its allegiance. An implacable warfare was begun by Pope Pius V., which had the result of convincing Englishmen that the Papacy was the determined foe of all that England held most dear. It was in the sphere of politics, rather than of religion, that Protestantism was stamped into the English mind.

The rising of the North was the result of this revival of Romanism. It seemed that Elizabeth's throne was doomed to fall before the forces which were gathering against it. The northern Earls, who were Romanists by conviction, thought that they could count upon Norfolk and his followers, who were ready to become Romanists through policy. That the movement failed so signally was due to Norfolk's vacillation, which robbed it of a pretext. A rising in favour of Norfolk's marriage with Mary might have been a plausible cry. When this was removed, the conspirators were at a loss for a definite statement of their objects. Westmoreland asked what the quarrel was to be, and was answered by a shout "For religion!" But he hesitated at the thought of undertaking the responsibility of introducing religious warfare into England. "Those," he said, "that seem to take that quarrel in other countries are counted as rebels; and I will never blot my name." The question then arose "whether by God's law they might wage battle against an anointed Prince, until he or she was lawfully excommunicated by the Head of the Church". Englishmen could not plead that they rose against intolerable oppression; and they were chary of admitting far-reaching principles which might recoil against themselves.

Doubtless the knowledge of this uncertainty weighed in some degree with Pope Pius V., and induced him to proceed to the excommunication of Elizabeth. It was a step which had long been urged on the Papacy by English refugees, who wished to proceed to extremities. Let the Church do its duty; then it would be seen who were on God's side. No harm could come of it, for the laws of England were merciful, and Parliament would not allow men to be put to death for their religion. So argued some of those who had presided over the fires of Smithfield. They were willing to use, for their own protection, the abhorrence of punishment for opinions which their own action had created in the breasts of Englishmen. But the Council of Trent did not feel strong enough to proceed openly against Elizabeth. The voice of politicians was against such a step when there were no means ready to give effect to the sentence. These motives of prudence did not weigh with the fiery and impetuous Pope Pius V., Michele Ghislieri, in whom the burning zeal of the sombre revival of Romanism was incarnated. His only thought was the recovery of the lost dominion of the Church, and its restoration to universal power. He was ready to expend all the treasures of the Church in a war against England. He dreamed of putting himself at the head of an expedition, and told some English refugees that he "wished he could pour out his blood for them". Without consulting the monarchs of his obedience, to know what help they would render, he issued a Bull declaring Elizabeth excommunicate, depriving her of her kingdom, absolving her people from their allegiance, and commanding them not to obey her commands or laws. At first, this Bull was kept secret and was sent to the Cardinal of Lorraine in

France for publication. On May 15, 1570, it was found nailed on the door of the Bishop of London's palace.

Elizabeth had already answered this Bull by anticipation. After the suppression of the rebellion she had addressed her people in a remarkable manifesto in which she appealed to them to judge between her and the stirrers of sedition. Nothing is more characteristic of Elizabeth than the frankness of this appeal to her people's intelligence, her willingness to explain to all the principles which she strove to enforce. The rebellion, she wrote, has failed; yet it is natural to consider why it happened. Partly it was due to the secret practices of malicious persons who played upon the fears of the northern Earls; partly it was due to the groundless fear of severity in respect to religious opinions; partly it gathered a vulgar herd who are always greedy of change. Yet the mass of the people stood firm, and she thanked them for their loyalty, in confirmation of which she wished to explain her past action and indicate her intentions about the future. "We do all persons to understand, that of our own natural disposition, we have always been desirous to have the obedience of all our subjects of all sorts, both high and low, by love and not by compulsion, by their own yielding and not by our exacting." She had ruled with clemency, and had not "sought the life, the blood, the goods, the houses, estates or lands of any person in any state or degree"; she had not acted for her own "revenge, profit, or pleasure". She had upheld the law, but in such way that the "judges criminal of the realm have in no time given fewer bloody judgments". She had engaged in no needless war, and had been more careful of her subjects' money than of her own; yet the realm had lost neither honour nor interest thereby. "We leave to all good and wise persons to consider, by way of comparison, what difference is to be found between the security, the tranquillity, the wealth, and all other worldly felicities, which our people do and may enjoy, and the continual and universal bloodsheds, burnings, spoilings, murders, exactions and such like, conjoined with civil wars in other countries."

She went on to consider the question of religion. "Occasion is sought, specially from foreign parts, to deprave this part of our Government, and consequently, by secret troubling the weak consciences of our people with untruths to withdraw them from obedience to our laws." She claimed no authority in matters ecclesiastical, save what had always been exercised by the English Crown. She had no power to determine any articles of the Christian faith, or to change any ceremony. But the Crown had authority "to direct all estates to live in the faith and obedience of the Christian religion, to see that the laws of God be duly observed, that offenders be duly punished, and consequently to provide that the Church be governed and taught by Archbishops, Bishops and Ministers, according to the ancient ecclesiastical policy of the realm, whom we do assist with our sovereign power. Yet, to answer malicious untruths, we have no meaning to allow that our subjects be molested either by examination or inquisition in any matter of faith, so long as they profess the Christian faith, not gainsaying the authority of Holy Scripture and of the articles of our faith contained in the Creeds, Apostolic and Catholic; or in any matter of ceremonies, so long as they shall, in their outward conversation, show themselves quiet and conformable, and not manifestly repugnant and obstinate to the laws of our realm, established for frequentation of Divine Service in the ordinary churches. If any potentate in Christendom, challenging any universal and sole superiority over the whole Church of Christ, as it is pretended, shall condemn this, our office by justice annexed to our Crown because it is not derived from his authority," Elizabeth was willing to submit the question to a free and general assembly. She was ready, "as a humble servant and handmaid of Christ, to reform herself and her policy in any manner, as truth shall guide and lead us. But truth is to be by us understood, known and received, as Almighty God shall please to reveal it, by His ordinary ways, and not to be in a disguised manner obtruded and forced by outward wars, or threatenings of bloodshed or such like curses, fulminations, or other worldly violences and practices; things unfit to be used for establishing or reforming of Christian religion, and to be rather contemned by Sovereign Princes having their seats and thrones established by Almighty God and not subject to the wills of foreign and strange usurped potentates."

It is worth while to contrast with this the preamble of Pius V.'s Bull. "He that reigneth on high, to Whom is ascribed all power, both in heaven and earth, hath committed the absolute government of His One, Holy, Catholic and Apostolic Church, outside of which there is no salvation, to only one upon earth, namely to Peter, the Chief of the Apostles, and to Peter's successor, the Bishop of Rome. Him alone has he made Prince, over all nations and kingdoms, to pluck up, destroy, scatter, consume, plant and build; that he may preserve the faithful, knit together in one common bond of charity, in the unity of the spirit, and present them safe and sound to their Saviour." Englishmen had before them two possibilities for the future: to accept the Papal claims, and make common cause with Spain and the Inquisition; or to uphold Elizabeth and maintain their national independence, with such large room for freedom of opinion as Elizabeth's government was prepared to give.

The immediate results of the excommunication were nothing. It was mere empty sound. The Pope had asserted his right to depose a heretical ruler; but the assertion did not affect Elizabeth's relations with those Powers who supported the Pope. No one was prepared to take any open action. Yet Elizabeth felt herself menaced and exposed to secret plots. The aspect of affairs grew sterner, and the fortunes of England were more closely united with the person of its Queen. The Romanists in England were marked out for suspicion, through no fault of their own. They were sacrificed wilfully to the pride and obstinacy of the Pope, who placed them theoretically in a position of disloyalty, which they did not wish to assume, but which they could not disavow.

The recognition of the Papal supremacy in things spiritual involved a political duty to deny the legitimacy of their Queen and
to disobey the law of their country.

These consequences were only slowly apparent. The immediate result was a series of bills brought into Parliament, in 1571,
for the protection of the Queen and the suppression of Papists.
The introduction of Papal Bulls into England, and the reconciling
of any Englishman to the Roman Church, were declared subject
to the penalties of high treason. So also was the assertion that the
Queen was "a heretic, schismatic, tyrant, infidel, or usurper of
the Crown," or the maintenance of the right of any other person,
or the discussion of the succession, except in Parliament. A Bill
was also passed requiring all persons to attend Church on Sun-
days, and to receive the Holy Communion at least twice a year.
To this Bill Elizabeth wisely refused her assent. Yet it was obvious that the temper of England had been stirred by the Pope's
action, which gave a serious check to the growing feeling in favour of freedom of opinion. It was not the fault of England, but
of the Papacy, that religion was confused with civil obedience
and that the recognition of the Papal supremacy involved treason
to the Queen. Legislation was drifting backwards, against men's
will and contrary to their better knowledge, because the Pope
was striving to bring upon England civil war and social destruction. To avert this a conception of legal uniformity in religion
grew in strength and gained a mischievous vitality.

It was not enough for Elizabeth to protect herself by laws;
she must also seek to check the designs of her enemies. She was
menaced by a joint invasion from France and Spain, which was
what the Pope longed to bring about. A pause in the religious
wars in France, in the middle of 1570, gave Charles IX. an opportunity to interfere for the liberation of Mary Queen of Scots.
Hitherto France had been busy with its own troubles; the prospect of peace meant a revival of jealousy of Spain. But France
could only be strong if it were united, and for that purpose the
Huguenots must be allowed a voice in affairs. For a time there

arose a project of a combination against Spain, and a partition of the Netherlands between France, England and Germany. In furtherance of this plan, the Huguenot leaders suggested a marriage between Elizabeth and the Duke of Anjou, Charles IX.'s younger brother. It is true that Anjou was only twenty and Elizabeth was thirty-seven; but this did not prevent a long negotiation being carried on in Paris by Francis Walsingham, a statesman trained by Cecil, who now first appears in public business. Neither Anjou nor Elizabeth desired the marriage in itself; but each was influenced by the possible advantages to be obtained. Anjou was reported "not averse to the religion" of England. Walsingham gave the Papal nuncio in Paris a copy of the English liturgy, "which form the Pope would have by a Council confirmed as Catholic, if the Queen would have acknowledged the same as received from him". How far Elizabeth was prepared to go it is impossible to say; but the negotiation was useful as preventing Anjou from being a candidate for the hand of Mary, and kept France from making common cause with Spain. But neither Anjou nor Elizabeth was prepared to enter on great undertakings. Anjou, at last, determined that he had a better career open to himself at home. With tears and protestations of devotion he refused to entertain the proposal in July, 1571, and his brother, the Duke of Alençon, was suggested in his stead.

This negotiation had the result of stirring the zeal of the Romanist conspirators in England. The Duke of Norfolk had been released from the Tower after solemnly signing a declaration that he would never again undertake any project for marrying Mary of Scotland, and would hold no further communication with her. He was still the head of the old nobles, who wished for certainty about the future, who had no confidence in Elizabeth's success, and saw their best hope in the marriage of Mary Stuart with Norfolk. There was resident in London an Italian banker, Ridolfi, ostensibly engaged in business, but really an agent of Pope Pius V. He proceeded to weave together again the broken threads of the conspiracy which had failed. He used the possibility of Elizabeth's marriage with Anjou as a means to work upon the unstable character of Norfolk. If he would privately declare himself a Romanist in religion, and would work with the Pope and Philip, they would help him to marry Mary. After some hesitation Norfolk accepted the proposal, and became a useful leader of an English party which could be used for other purposes than it was aware of. An English rising, supported by Alva from the Netherlands, and favoured by the English nobles, would indeed prove formidable. Ridolfi went to Brussels to lay his plan before Alva, and thence went to Spain to obtain Philip's sanction. Both Alva and Philip were of opinion that the assassination of Elizabeth was the first step to be taken; then would come the English rising and the Spanish help. It is some credit to Englishmen to know that at that time there was no one among them who could be suggested as likely to attempt the Queen's life. An Italian volunteered for the purpose.

The means by which this plot was discovered gives a curious insight into the watchfulness of Cecil, and the methods of an English minister in that agitated time. The population of England was so small, scarcely three millions, that it was possible for a minister to have a personal knowledge of all men of any importance. Cecil received from all officials, in Church and State, reports about the religious and political opinions and attitude of all who dwelt within their districts. Suspicious actions were at once known to him; and he had organised a system of spies, whose sagacity he might trust. It was necessary to check conspiracies in their beginning, and Cecil was ever watchful for that purpose. The seaports were especially guarded, and letters from abroad were watched for. Though Cecil had no suspicion of Ridolfi, he suspected that some plot would probably be hatched, and redoubled his measures of precaution. Ridolfi sent from Brussels a messenger with letters to Mary's ambassador, the Bishop of Ross, and also to the Duke of Norfolk and Lord Lumley. The messenger's baggage was searched, and the letters were discovered. These were first taken to the Warden of the Cinque Ports, who, desirous of screening the Duke of Norfolk, allowed the Bishop of Ross to substitute for them some other papers, less compromising to individuals, before sending the packet to Cecil. Still Cecil's suspicions were awakened, and Ridolfi's messenger was sent to the Tower, where he was thrown into the company of a pretended prisoner, and apparently a sympathiser, who was really a spy of Cecil's. From his admissions, which were reported to Cecil, it was clear that more was to be discovered, and the Bishop of Ross was next examined and put under custody.

It happened that, about this time, Sir John Hawkins had devised a scheme of his own for hoodwinking Philip. In his disastrous expedition to the Indies he had lost several of his ships, and grieved over the thought that many of his trusty comrades were lying in Spanish dungeons as prisoners of war. He paid a visit to the Spanish ambassador, Don Guerau d'Espes, and professed himself sorely discontented with the treatment which he had received from the Queen. He hinted that, if his men were restored, he might be willing to abandon the service of Elizabeth for that of Philip, and carry with him the best of the English seamen. Mary Queen of Scots was secretly asked to join her prayers with those of Hawkins, who was consequently able to win Philip's confidence and penetrate to some degree into the plot which was on foot. Thus, in the middle of 1571, Cecil knew that a treasonable correspondence was passing between the Bishop of Ross and the Netherlands, and that Philip was projecting an invasion of England in behalf of Mary Queen of Scots. Still this was all concerned with foreign affairs. There was nothing to inculpate any one in England, till an accident gave Cecil a further clue.

In September a sum of money was entrusted to the Duke of Norfolk to forward to Scotland for the use of Mary's partisans. It was given to a merchant to carry to Shrewsbury. Struck with the weight of the bag, he opened it and found a letter in cipher, which he sent to Lord Burghley (for Cecil had been raised to the peerage), who imprisoned the Duke's servants, threatened them with torture, and discovered the key to the cipher. The Duke

was imprisoned, and was examined from time to time, as Burghley discovered more from his servants and unearthed his correspondence. Little by little the whole plot was cleared up. "This
matter of the Duke of Norfolk grows daily larger upon examination," wrote Burghley; "I am sorry to see so many touched therewith." Indeed, both Elizabeth and her minister had cause to feel
alarmed at the extent of disaffection which was revealed among
the nobles. It was thought better not to inquire too far, and only
to make an example of the chief offenders. The Bishop of Ross
was kept in the Tower till it was thought safe to allow him to
retire to France. The Spanish ambassador was requested to return
to Spain. Norfolk was brought to trial before a Court composed
of twenty-six peers. It was hard to find amongst the English
nobles a sufficient number of those who were not, in some degree
or other, accomplices of his projects. In January, 1572, Norfolk
was condemned as guilty of high treason by the president of the
Court, the Earl of Shrewsbury, who, with tears running down his
cheeks, pronounced sentence of death against the chief member
of his own order.

Yet, though Norfolk was condemned, Elizabeth hesitated to
sign the warrant for his execution. She was averse from bloodshed, and valued the popularity which goes with a reputation for
clemency. Once, when she was induced to sign the warrant, and
the day of Norfolk's execution was fixed, she sent for Burghley,
told him she could not bear the thought of Norfolk's death, and
commanded a respite. Her friends were amazed at her carelessness for her personal safety, as shown in her reluctance to punish
the man who had by his treason exposed her to assassination.
"The world knows her to be wise," wrote Lord Hunsdon, "and
surely there cannot be a greater point of wisdom than for any to
be careful of their own estate, and especially the preservation of
their own life. How much more needful is it for Her Majesty to
take heed, upon whose life depends a whole commonwealth, the
utter ruin of the whole country, and the utter subversion of religion? If by her negligence or womanish pity these things happen,

what she hath to answer for to God, she herself knows." Still Elizabeth refused to act till Parliament met, in May, and uttered its opinion with no uncertain voice. It resolved in the first place to attaint Mary Queen of Scots and so "touch her in life as well as in title". It was weary of Elizabeth's endless negotiations about restoring Mary to Scotland, and recognising her right of succession. It longed to make an end of the perpetual dangers to which the country was exposed for her sake. But Elizabeth insisted that the attainder should be dropped. She declared that "she could not put to death the bird that had flown to her for succour from the hawk". The Commons replied that there was no other course open; to pass a bill excluding her from the succession would admit her right and make her friends more desperate. Elizabeth assented, but asked them to let the matter stand over. Disappointed of their chief desire, the Commons besought the immediate execution of the Duke of Norfolk. To this Elizabeth reluctantly consented, and the Duke's head fell on Tower Hill on June 2.

With his death another period of Elizabeth's reign was marked. She had successfully withstood the first shock of the Romanist revival. The rising of the North was an outburst of dissatisfaction at home. The Ridolfi plot was a deep-laid scheme for bringing to bear on England all the resources of the old religion. It had failed, and even the attempt had revealed an inherent weakness in the combination. There was no talk of help from France, which had begun to draw nearer to England through hostility to Spain. Its national interest was stronger than its religious interest. There was even a hope of a confederacy in which France and England should take part to check the growth of Spanish power by rescuing the Netherlands from its clutches. This large scheme halted; but, in April, 1572, a treaty was made between England and France, in which nothing was said about Mary Stuart, and the two countries undertook to aid each other in case of attack on any pretext whatever.

It was and must always remain a problem, what would have

been the results on European history if Elizabeth had been capable of a bold policy; and at no time is the question more interesting than just at this period of her reign. The Huguenot leaders in France had gained great influence over the King and were urging religious conciliation and war against Spain. If Elizabeth had been willing to marry the Duke of Anjou and so give England's support to this project, a decisive effort would have been possible. It is natural for the historian, wearied with the endless records of plans which came to nothing, to wish for something which might aim at decision. It is easy to arrange on paper what might have happened, if all had gone well. But Elizabeth could count what she had gained by waiting on events, and shrunk from great schemes. France became convinced that Elizabeth would not join in war against Spain in the Netherlands, and hesitated to engage in it alone. Yet things had gone so far that it was hard to withdraw. "Your Lordship seeth," wrote Walsingham from Paris, "how the fruit of your fear there hath bred fear here: whereof I fear there will follow fearful effects, unless God put to His helping hand." The "fearful effects," which Walsingham foresaw, was the massacre of St. Bartholomew's Day, which filled England with horror.

At first men thought that it was a signal for a general murder of all Protestants, and there was universal alarm. When this subsided the rage against France was extreme; but Elizabeth was loath to part with her new ally. She devised a dignified plan for satisfying the popular indignation in an impressive fashion. When the French ambassador pressed for an interview, Elizabeth received him at Woodstock, with her Council around her, all dressed in deep mourning. The ambassador entered amid solemn silence, and his excuses were coldly listened to. Elizabeth said that she had purposed sending an embassy to France: she could trust no one in a country where life was unsafe. Burghley followed, saying that it was the most horrible crime committed since the Crucifixion. Yet, after making this protest, Elizabeth consented to be godmother to the daughter of Charles IX., and sent the Earl of

Worcester as her proxy. Some Englishmen were so indignant at this that his boat was attacked by a privateer in the Channel, and several of his men were killed in the encounter.

Elizabeth was prospering by the misfortunes of others. She could compare the results of her caution with those of the great schemes of other rulers, and could find consolation in the comparison. Spain, with all its apparent strength, was harassed by the revolt of the Netherlands; no sooner were the rebels reduced on land than a new and more difficult warfare arose on sea, by the rise of the "Water Beggars," with Brill and Flushing for their harbours. France, divided between religious discord and fear of Philip, had no clear policy to pursue. Spain and France alike had need of England's friendship, and left to the Pope the task of reducing that heretical country to obedience. In Scotland the capture of the Castles of Dumbarton and Edinburgh reduced Mary's party to helplessness. At the end of 1572 Elizabeth could look around her with greater confidence; and the country entered upon a period of peace, during which its commerce and its naval power steadily increased.

Some token of the rising influence of commerce in England is to be found in the project of Sir Thomas Gresham for the improvement of the means by which business was conducted. Gresham had been employed in the Low Countries to negotiate loans for the State, and had made a princely fortune for himself while so doing. The death of his only son turned his mind towards civic munificence, and he offered to build for the city of London an Exchange, such as he had often frequented at Antwerp. Hitherto in England business was transacted in the street, or in the nave of St. Paul's Cathedral. Gresham built a quadrangle, with a portico for merchants' warehouses beneath, and shops above. In January, 1571, he asked the Queen to open it. She came in state, and after dining with Gresham in his house in Bishopsgate Street, visited the new building, and bade the herald proclaim its name as the Royal Exchange. It is worth noticing that Gresham knew how to derive advantage from the royal visit. His shops were unlet; and though the building was there it was not immediately possible to overcome old habits and ensure its success. So Gresham visited the chief shopkeepers and asked them to expose some of their goods in the empty windows, and kindle a few candles in honour of the Queen's coming: they might keep the shops rent free for a year. He rightly calculated that, when once they were there, they would not withdraw from a place which their coming had made central; and he was able to obtain a good rental for his shops in the following year.

Elizabeth herself was by no means entirely absorbed with State affairs, difficult as they were. She was endowed with a strong and many-sided nature, and was full of vitality. She threw off business and frankly enjoyed herself according to her liking. "Her humours did not grow weak with age;" she became more and more imperious and exacting to those around her. She was easy of access and ready of speech, but no one was allowed to forget that she was a Queen. In State affairs she mainly trusted to Burghley; but in private life she chose her own companions, not for their merits but for their social gifts. Leicester still retained his place in her favour, but there were others beside him. A young lawyer from Northamptonshire, Christopher Hatton, attracted her attention by his graceful dancing at a masque, and rapidly won his way to close intimacy. She called him her "Mutton," her "Bellwether," her "pecora campi". When he fell ill, in 1573, she visited him daily; and when he was ordered to Spa for his health she sent her own physician to accompany him. His letters on the journey breathed the most extravagant devotion. "My spirit," he wrote, "agreeth with my body and life that to serve you is a heaven, but to lack you is more than hell's torment with them. Would to God that I were with you but for one hour. My wits are overwrought with thoughts. I find myself amazed. Passion overcometh me. I can write no more. Love me, for I love you." He signs himself "Your most unhappy bondsman, Lyddes," another of the Queen's nicknames for him. Another example of his style is the following: "This is the twelfth day since I saw the brightness of that sun that giveth light unto my sense and soul. I was an amazed creature. Give me leave, madam, to remove myself out of this irksome shadow so far as my imagination with their good means may lead me towards you: and let me thus salute you: Live for ever, most excellent creature, and love some man to show yourself thankful for God's high labour in you." And this was written to Elizabeth when she was of the age of forty!

We have an interesting picture of the Court life at this time in a letter of Gilbert Talbot to his father, the Earl of Shrewsbury, who was kept away from London by his duties as gaoler of Mary Queen of Scots. Few things are more characteristic of Elizabeth's methods of government than her capacity of attaching men to her service by compelling them to undertake difficult and thankless duties. The great Earl of Shrewsbury, because his estates lay in the safe region of the Midlands, alike out of the reach of Scottish raids and of a sudden dash for rescue from the east coast, was bidden by the Queen to entertain Mary. At first she was an honoured guest, soon to be returned to her own land. But years went by and Shrewsbury was still saddled with his unwelcome charge. She was transferred from one to another of his many residences according as need required. He was turned from her host to her keeper; and Elizabeth's demands upon his care grew more and more exacting. Between two imperious women his life was made a burden to him; but there was no escape from his task, in which his honour and his fortunes were alike involved. He could only sigh for relief and solace himself in his enforced retirement by receiving political news from Burghley and gossip from his son. Talbot wrote to his father in May, 1573:—

"My Lord Treasurer (Burghley), even after the old manner dealeth with matters of State only, and beareth himself very uprightly. My Lord Leicester is very much with Her Majesty, and she shows the same great affection to him that she was wont; of late he has endeavoured to please her more than heretofore. There are two sisters now in the Court that are very far in love with him, as they have been long, my Lady Sheffield and Frances

Howard (daughters of Lord Howard of Effingham). They, of like striving who shall love him better, are at great wars together, and the Queen thinketh not well of them, and not better of him: by this means there are spies over him. My Lord of Sussex goes with the tide and helps to back others; but his own credit is sober, considering his estate; he is very diligent in his office (Lord Chamberlain) and takes great pains. My Lord of Oxford is lately grown into great credit: for the Queen's Majesty delighteth more in his personage, and his dancing, and valiantness, than any other. I think Sussex doth back him all that he can; if it were not for his fickle head he would pass any of them shortly. My Lady Burghley unwisely has declared herself as it were jealous, which has come to the Queen's ear; whereat she had been not a little offended at her, but now she is reconciled again. At all their love matters my Lord Treasurer winketh, and will not meddle anyway." It is a curious picture which is here given of a capricious woman, who deliberately bestowed her favours on purely personal grounds, and chose for her associates those who were not fitted to interfere in affairs of State. She contrived to set them one against another, and so prevented the growth of parties. Success was possible to any one, but no one could establish a claim. Elizabeth was glad to see her courtiers vieing for her favour; if some of them were treacherous it was the more necessary to attach them to herself. They were allured to the Court, and were induced to commit themselves to her side. Behind those who fluttered round the Court were the political instruments of her government, well trained by Burghley, and the growing circle of those related to her on her mother's side, such as Lord Hunsdon, on whom she could depend for help at a crisis. Her real servants were kept in the background. She would be Queen over all her people, and was anxious that her Court should be representative of all shades of opinion.

So, partly from liking, and partly from policy, she indulged in outward splendour, and encouraged those whose taste lay in that direction. In May, 1571, jousts were held at Westminster, in which the challengers were the Earl of Oxford, Sir Charles Howard, Sir Henry Lee, and Sir Christopher Hatton. Lee was the most accomplished knight in the tilt-yard, and founded a society of Knights-Tilters, who were to appear as challengers on each anniversary of the Queen's accession. Edward de Vere, Earl of Oxford, was one of the gayest, but was certainly the most brutal of Elizabeth's courtiers. He married Burghley's daughter Anne, and tried to use his influence in politics to save his relative the Duke of Norfolk. When he failed he avenged himself on Burghley by ill-treating his wife; but neither his treasons nor his misconduct induced Elizabeth to exclude him from her presence.

Nor did Elizabeth only care to attach the nobles to her person. She was careful to maintain her popularity among her people. Her progresses, or summer journeys, answered both purposes. She was entertained by the nobles, and her presence in any district was an occasion for revels in which the whole neighbourhood took part. Civic officials welcomed the Queen and were delighted with her condescension. She listened to interminable harangues, with inexhaustible patience, and always found a happy compliment in reply. Thus, at Warwick, she called the Recorder: "Come hither, little Recorder. It was told me that you would be afraid to look on me or to speak boldly; but you were not so afraid of me as I was of you, and I now thank you for putting me in mind of my duty." The greatest occasion of display was the Queen's visit to the Earl of Leicester at Kenilworth Castle, in the summer of 1575. The records of it suffice to show that Leicester was a consummate courtier, and knew how to captivate imagination of all beholders. The pageantry, which was devised with laborious care, shows us the pedantry of the English Renaissance period, modelled on that of Italy, but marked with sturdy characteristics of its own. Bold and extravagant as it seems to us, it was the foundation on which arose the English drama. The rude and affected style of its allegorical representations only needed to be chastened and brought into connection with life and character. We wonder if, amongst the lookers-on, a young lad of the name of William Shakespeare had been brought from Warwick by his parents and feasted his eyes on the splendid scene.

Elizabeth was met by Leicester and entertained at dinner seven miles away on the borders of his domains. Thence the Royal party advanced slowly, hunting by the way. It was eight o'clock on a summer's evening when the battlements of Kenilworth Castle came in view. Before the first gate ten sibyls, clad in white silk, welcomed the Queen with a long poem in English. As she approached the gate a huge porter rushed forward, brandishing a gigantic club, denouncing in uncouth language the bustle and stir which disturbed his wonted repose. But when his eyes fell on the Queen his weapon dropped from his hand; he yielded up his keys and kneeling, prayed for pardon of his impatience; then he bade the trumpeters on the wall to sound. Six giants, eight feet high, all clad in silk, blew from silver trumpets a blast of welcome as Elizabeth passed through the tilt-ground to the pool which ran in front of the castle. There, on a movable island blazing with torches, sat the Lady of the Lake, who rehearsed how she had kept the waters since King Arthur's days, but now resigned her charge to the Queen. After receiving this submission Elizabeth proceeded along a bridge thrown over the old moat, seventy feet long, adorned with pillars on which stood bowls containing the appropriate offerings of the rural deities, the meaning of which was explained by a poet, clad in sky-blue silk, with a garland of laurel round his brow. After listening to all this flow of poetry the Queen was allowed to approach the door and dismount from her horse. The rest of the evening was enlivened by a great display of fireworks in the courtyard.

It were long to tell of all that happened of like sort during the nineteen days of the Queen's sojourn. As she hunted in the forest the Wild Man of the Woods rushed out to inquire who she was, and his bellowings were answered by an ingenious echo. There was bear-baiting, and tumbling, and rustic sports. There was a country wedding, and a play acted by the men of Coventry; there were songs and masques, Mermaids and Tritons swam in the pool, and expressed appropriate loyalty. Arion rode a dolphin which contained within it an orchestra of six men who accompanied his patriotic songs. At some time or another all the Gods of the mythology had an opportunity of saying their say and used it to the full. Elizabeth must have departed with the assurance that she was the special care of Olympus.

Elizabeth herself was infected with the poetical fury of the times, as the following sonnet shows. It must have been written soon after Norfolk's execution:—

> *The dread of future foes exiles my present joy,*
> *And wit me warns to shun such snares as threaten mine*
>   *annoy.*
> *For falsehood now doth flow, and subjects' faith doth ebb;*
> *Which would not be if Reason ruled, or Wisdom weaved*
>   *the web.*
> *But clouds of toys untried do cloak aspiring minds,*
> *Which turn to rain of late repent by course of changed*
>   *winds.*
> *The top of hope supposed the root of ruth will be,*
> *And fruitless all their graffed guiles, as shortly ye shall see.*
> *Those dazzled eyes with pride, which great ambition*
>   *blinds,*
> *Shall be unsealed by worthy wights whose foresight*
>   *falsehood finds.*
> *The Daughter of Debate, that eke discord doth sow,*
> *Shall reap no gain where former rule hath taught still peace*
>   *to grow*
> *No foreign banished wight shall anchor in this port;*
> *Our realm it brooks no stranger's force, let them elsewhere*
>   *resort.*
> *Our rusty sword with rest shall first his edge employ,*
> *To poll their tops that seek such change and gape for joy.*

But though the country was at peace, and growing rapidly in prosperity, Elizabeth did not forget her watchfulness amidst her amusements. The thought of "the Daughter of Debate," Queen Mary, was never absent from her mind, and she was never sure that she could entirely trust any one. At the end of 1574 she was greatly disturbed by the news that Lord Charles Stuart, Darnley's younger brother, had secretly married Elizabeth Cavendish, daughter of Lady Shrewsbury by a former marriage. As Shrewsbury was the guardian of Queen Mary it betokened that intrigues were going on to attach him, if possible, to Mary's party, but Elizabeth did not know to whom she could more safely entrust Mary, and was silent. As it happened, Lord Charles and his wife both died within a year, leaving a daughter, the luckless Arabella Stuart. Even Burghley was at times an object of the Queen's suspicion. He went for two successive years to Buxton to take the waters, and wrote afterwards to Shrewsbury: "Her Majesty did conceive that my being there was, by means of your Lordship and my Lady, to enter into intelligence with the Queen of Scots. And hereof, on my return to Her Majesty's presence, I had very sharp reproofs for my going to Buckstones, with plain charging of me for favouring the Queen of Scots; and that in so earnest a sort as I never looked for, knowing my integrity to Her Majesty."

Two years later Leicester paid a visit to Buxton and was entertained at Chatsworth by Lord and Lady Shrewsbury. Elizabeth expressed her disapproval in a sarcastic letter, which is strangely characteristic of her complicated way of expressing her wishes. She wrote: "Being given to understand from our cousin, the Earl of Leicester, how honourably he was lately received by you and our cousin, the Countess, at Chatsworth, and how his diet is by you both discharged at Buxton, we should do him great wrong, holding him in that place in our favour in which we do, in case we should not let you understand in how thankful sort we accept the same at your hands; which we do not acknowledge to be done unto him but to our own self; and therefore do mean to take upon us the debt and to acknowledge you both as our creditors, so as you can be content to accept us for debtor; wherein is danger, unless you cut off some part of the large allowance of diet you give him, lest otherwise the debt thereby may grow to be so great as we shall not be able to discharge the same, and so become bankrupt. And therefore, we think it, for the saving of our credit, meet to prescribe unto you a proportion of diet which we mean in no case you shall exceed; and that is, to allow him by the day for his meat two ounces of flesh, referring the quality to yourselves, so as you exceed not the quantity; and for his drink the twentieth part of a pint of wine to comfort his stomach, and as much of St. Anne's sacred water as he listeth to drink. On festival days, as is meet for a man of his quality, we can be content you enlarge his diet by allowing unto him for his dinner the shoulder of a wren, and for his supper a leg of the same besides his ordinary ounces."

Elizabeth's progress in Norfolk, in 1578, afforded unmistakable signs of the growth of trade, and consequent prosperity. The religious troubles had driven many of the Flemings from their homes. They settled chiefly in Norwich, and set up their looms for weaving fine cloth. From these exiles England learned the beginning of its manufacturing industry. In Norwich, at all events, men understood their debt to Elizabeth's careful government, and their gratitude was genuine. The Mayor presented the Queen with a large cup, containing a hundred pounds. Elizabeth lifted the cover, and said to the footmen to whose charge she committed it: "Look to it: there is a hundred pounds". She was sure that in a commercial city her carefulness would be duly appreciated. Amid the pageants with which she was greeted, one at least was instinct with reality. Upon a stage were eight girls spinning yarn, and eight others knitting the yarn into hose: between the two groups stood a boy attired to represent the city, who addressed the Queen in verses which spoke the literal truth:—

> *Most gracious Prince, undoubted sovereign Queen,*
> *Our only joy next God, and chief defence:*
> *In this small show our whole estate is seen,*
> *The wealth we have we find proceeds from thence*
> *The idle hand here hath no place to feed,*
> *The painful wight hath still to serve his need.*

Again, our seat denies us traffic here,
    The sea too near divides us from the rest;
So weak we were within this dozen year
    As care did quench the courage of the best,
But good advice hath taught these little hands
To rend in twain the force of pining bands.

From combed wool we draw this slender thread,
    From thence the looms have dealing with the same,
And thence again, in order to proceed,
    These several works which skilful art doth frame;
And all to drive dame Need into her cave
Our hearts and hands together laboured have.

We bought before the things which now we sell;
    These slender imps their works do pass the waves;
God's peace and thine we hold, and prosper well;
    Of every mouth the hands the charges saves,
Thus through thy help, and aid of power divine,
Doth Norwich live, whose hearts and goods are thine.

These homely verses tell the tale of the change which was passing over the industrial life of England. A few years before, the finest wool was exported to the Netherlands, there to be woven and dyed; and England's foreign trade mostly lay in raw material. Now it was rapidly taking into its own hands the process of manufacture, and a new prospect opened before it. The men of Norwich were justified in expressing a proud sense of the industrial growth of England, selling the wares which once it bought, exporting over the seas the workmanship of its children; they rejoiced that the labour of the hands could supply the needs of life, and they recognised that this was due to the Queen's wisdom and prudence, which had secured for the country the blessings of peace. Her visit to Norwich must have compensated Elizabeth for many struggles, and apologised for many insincerities. She saw there the practical results of her difficult and complicated policy.

V

THE ALENÇON MARRIAGE

~§ The peace which England enjoyed depended on her combination with France to keep Philip employed in the Netherlands. The loose conception of international relations which then prevailed made it possible for these two countries to throw many hindrances in the way of the subjugation of the revolted provinces. English privateers preyed upon the Spanish traders in the Channel, and rendered communications between Spain and the Netherlands unsafe by sea. France could supply volunteers by land without any open declaration of war. But this attitude of France depended on some hopes of future gain, and was only possible so long as there was a party which could give these hopes a definite expression. After the massacre of St. Bartholomew's Day the only man who seemed fitted to carry on the Huguenot policy was the King's youngest brother, the Duke of Alençon. He was unhappy in the Court, and was full of adventurous aspirations. When the plan of Elizabeth's marriage with Anjou fell to the ground, Alençon was substituted in his brother's stead. At first this was merely a polite way of covering Anjou's withdrawal, but Alençon's imagination was captivated at the prospect. He saw in it the possibilities of a career, and seriously set to work to realise them.

At the end of 1572 he sent to England a Huguenot gentleman, Maisonfleur, who made fantastic proposals, and communicated them in equally fantastic language. In his correspondence Elizabeth was Madame de Lisle, and Alençon was Don Lucidor. The marriage was, in his eyes, a romance of chivalry, and he proposed that Alençon should flee from Paris and come to England as a fugitive Prince in quest of a peerless bride. As Elizabeth was now

forty years old, and Alençon little more than twenty, this attempt at sentiment was ridiculous. Moreover, Alençon was
scarcely suited to the part of a fairy prince. He was short in
stature, with a face marked with small-pox, and further disfigured
with a swollen nose. He was more prudent than his envoy, and
refused to leave France without some invitation from Elizabeth,
who refused to bestow her affections on a man whom she had not
seen, and whose reputation for beauty was doubtful. Maisonfleur
rebuked her hesitation. "It were expedient, Madam," he wrote,
"that you thought less of mere corporal beauty, provided that the
work of God be done." Elizabeth professed to wish to be assured
of Alençon's good intentions. He was warring against the
Huguenots: let the King of France make peace and abandon the
siege of La Rochelle. Charles IX. wished for nothing better than
peace and the departure of his troublesome brother. He accepted
Elizabeth's conditions; but Alençon did not flee to England. The
King was ill, and there was a Huguenot plot to seize the opportunity for a rising. It was discovered, and Alençon was put in
prison, where he remained till Charles died in 1574. After the
accession of Henry III. he escaped and joined the Huguenot
army, but was driven to make peace with his brother in 1576.

Meanwhile Elizabeth had lost all hope that the Netherlands
would make good their revolt from Spain. She would not help
them herself, and she dreaded their possession by France as much
as their possession by Spain. She seems to have thought it wisest
to repress French interference, and allow the rebellion to smoul-
der out, so that no definite crisis might arise in connection with
it. If she took any decided part it might involve her in war with
Spain. So she fed the Prince of Orange with promises and gave
him encouragement to continue the struggle, but refused any material help when help was sorely needed. In the same way she
seems to have resolved to play with Alençon, who had before
him the alternatives of making himself a position in the Netherlands or in England. Elizabeth was determined that he should do
neither. When he thought of Flanders she encouraged his hopes

on England; when he listened to her encouragement she allured him with expectations which she never meant to satisfy.

It was a dangerous game, but one for which Elizabeth was well fitted; and it had all the elements of reckless adventure which, in personal matters, she keenly enjoyed. So when, in 1578, Alençon went to help the Netherlands, she intimated to him that his proposals would be favourably received in England. Alençon sent envoys who clearly stated that, as he was ill-used at home, he must make his fortunes elsewhere; he was resolved either to marry Elizabeth or win the crown of the Netherlands; he hoped to combine both. As a matter of fact, Alençon knew that he had not the means to maintain his forces in the Netherlands. His negotiations with Elizabeth might be useful to make him a more influential personage and reconcile him with his brother. He was a political adventurer, and was playing a game with Elizabeth in the same way as she was playing a game with him. So long as the Alençon marriage was under discussion she could defer any decision about a policy towards the Netherlands. To avoid decisive action had now become a habit to which she clung with tenacious pertinacity. By confounding the personal question of her marriage with the political question of helping the Netherlands she was able to keep matters in her own hands without giving a reason to the remonstrances of her advisers. She seized the opportunity, and used it to the full. She made a great show of activity which ended in nothing.

First Elizabeth required that Alençon should leave the Netherlands, and suggested that he should pay her a visit in England. Before committing himself he sent a gentleman of his household, Simier, to survey the ground. Simier arrived in January, 1579, and was received with great marks of favour. To the annoyance of Leicester he became the Queen's pet and plaything; she called him her "petit singe". When a lady of the chamber suggested that Leicester would make a better husband than Alençon, Elizabeth angrily asked: "Do you think me so unmindful of my Royal dignity as to prefer my servant, whom I myself have raised, to the greatest Prince in Christendom?" Matters seemed to Simier to be advancing, and there was a general belief that the Queen was in earnest. The marriage was not popular, and a preacher in the Chapel Royal boldly said that England could not endure a second foreign marriage after its experience of Queen Mary; whereupon Elizabeth angrily rose and left the chapel. Alençon's proposals were submitted to the Council, who after a long deliberation told Simier that his terms could not be accepted. Simier carried his sorrow to the Queen, who swore that the Council should not hinder her; she was resolved to marry. But she used this opposition of the Council to tell Alençon that he must wait a while; let them be friends, and their friendship might grow.

But Alençon was tired of waiting and pressed for an invitation to England. While Elizabeth hesitated to send him a passport, Simier suddenly informed her of Leicester's marriage to the widowed Countess of Essex. It would seem that Leicester, despairing of his marriage with the Queen, and notorious for his love affairs with other ladies, was at last forced into matrimony. His connection with Lady Essex was of long standing; and, after her husband's death, her father, Sir Francis Knollys, was resolved to protect the honour of his daughter. Leicester gave way, and the marriage was secretly performed in September, 1578. Simier penetrated the secret and made use of it. Elizabeth, at first, was furious, commanded Leicester to confine himself to his house at Greenwich, and spoke of committing him to the Tower. But wiser councils prevailed, and Leicester was soon pardoned. Simier accused him of seeking to revenge himself by an attempt on his life, and special measures were taken for his protection. Soon after, as Elizabeth was in her barge on the river, in Simier's company, a shot was fired which struck one of the rowers on the arm. The culprit was discovered; but it seemed a misadventure, and the Queen would exact no punishment. She was never deficient in personal courage, and refused to entertain suspicions. She was wont to say that she would believe nothing against her people which a father would not believe against his children.

The end of all this was that Simier obtained permission for Alençon to pay England a visit in August, 1579. He came privately and only stayed a few days, during which he scarcely went outside the palace. Elizabeth expressed herself quite satisfied with her suitor, in spite of his unprepossessing appearance. She called him her "grenouille," and professed to find hidden merits which promised well for the future. Alençon departed well pleased with his reception and full of hope.

In fashionable circles the betting was three to one that the marriage would not take place; but it was natural that the people, ignorant of political intrigues, should be disturbed at the notion of a French marriage. A token of this was given by a pamphlet written by a Puritan lawyer, John Stubbs, the title of which sufficiently indicates its contents. It was called "The Discovery of the Gaping Gulf, whereinto England is likely to be swallowed by a French marriage, if the Lord forbid not the banns, by letting Her Majesty see the sin and punishment thereof". It was written in the plain language of honest conviction, and spoke out home truths. Elizabeth was too old to marry, as there was little hope of issue; nor was Alençon a man of good character. England had nothing to gain and everything to fear from such a marriage. Elizabeth was furious at such discussion of her private affairs. She had always demanded that her subjects should leave her a free hand, and she resented plain speaking. It was in her eyes dangerous that the ignorant should meddle in matters that they could not understand. She issued a proclamation in defence of Alençon, who was slandered simply because he had shown his affection for her. Her subjects had ever been persuading her to marry: as soon as she took a step to meet their wishes she was treated with unworthy reproaches. The author and printer of the pamphlet were committed to the Tower, and Elizabeth determined to wreak condign vengeance. At first she threatened to have them hanged; but it was difficult to frame an indictment. Ultimately proceedings were taken under an Act passed in Mary's reign for the protection of the Queen's husband. The accused were condemned to

suffer the loss of their right hands, "though some lawyers muttered that the sentence was erroneous and void," because the Act
was only passed for the protection of Philip, and expired with
Mary's death. One who so murmured was committed to the
Tower; and one of the judges, who held his view, "was so sharply
reprehended that he resigned his place". The savage sentence was
carried out. Stubbs and his printer had their right hands cut off
on a scaffold at Westminster. A butcher's knife was driven
through their wrist with a mallet. Stubbs, after his right hand had
been severed, waved his hat with his left, and cried "God save the
Queen". We do not wonder that the "multitude standing about
was deeply silent, either out of horror at this new and unwonted
punishment, or else out of commiseration towards the man, as
being of honest repute, or else out of hatred of the marriage,
which most men presaged would be the overthrow of religion".
Elizabeth's crooked schemes were leading her to suppress public
opinion by savagery. She was averse to shed the blood of conspicuous persons, but she had no such objection to the punishment of those of meaner sort. While she was careful to secure her
popularity by affability, she sternly repressed any expression of
opinion which ran counter to her plans.

But though Elizabeth might muzzle her people, she could not
silence her counsellors, amongst whom only the Earl of Sussex
was in favour of the marriage. Burghley was willing to give way
to the Queen's wishes; perhaps he suspected their sincerity. The
other nobles were almost unanimous in their objections. Philip
Sidney, a young man of twenty-four, who had everything to gain
from the Queen's favour, expressed his opinion against the marriage as steadfastly as Stubbs had done, though within the limits
of good taste and fair argument. Alençon would undermine the
English Church and introduce confusion; he would "banish free
spirits and faithful patriots till the ideas of native freedom should
be utterly forgotten"; he would disturb foreign relationships by
aggrandising France. Elizabeth could not answer Sidney as she
had answered Stubbs; but her favourite, the Earl of Oxford,

thought that he would please her by a display of insolence. He picked a quarrel with Sidney in the tennis-court, and called him a "puppy". Sidney gave him the lie and waited for a challenge. When none came, he sent to ask if his French friends could not teach him the rules of honour among gentlemen. But the Council forbade fighting, and referred the matter to the Queen, who patched up the quarrel. Sidney, however, felt himself bound to maintain his opinions and addressed a dignified letter to Elizabeth in which he set forward all the objections which he entertained to the proposed marriage.

Elizabeth seemed unmoved by argument, even when the Lords of the Council waited on her and spoke in the same strain. She poured out her rage on Walsingham; then she burst into tears, and said that she was only desirous of doing what was best for the realm, "to marry and have a child and continue the line of her father"; she had expected that every one would approve of her laudable purpose. The Council again discussed the matter, and returned to say that they would die at her feet rather than offend her; if her mind was made up they would do as she wished. Elizabeth received their submission with sulky ill-humour, and repaid their devotion with jibes and reproaches. She seemed quite resolute. On November 24, 1579, the marriage treaty was drawn up and signed by Simier; it only needed the sanction of Parliament. But here was a difficulty. The pamphlet of Stubbs and his severe sentence had stirred men's minds, and the temper of Parliament could not be trusted. It was obvious that the matter must wait a while; so Simier agreed to a delay of two months in which the Queen was to persuade her subjects.

Two months passed, and nothing was done. Alençon had been withdrawn from the Netherlands, and a marriage between him and the daughter of Philip II. had been put aside. Perhaps Elizabeth thought that result worth all the trouble she had taken; and she pursued her tortuous course. Burghley besought her to make up her mind. "If you mean to marry," he said, "do so at once; if not, undeceive the Duke of Alençon." "Others," said Elizabeth, "advise me to entertain him with half-promises." "Madam," answered Burghley, "there is a proverb that those who fool princes fool themselves." But Elizabeth had boundless confidence in her capacity for fooling others without paying the penalty, and Alençon was kept waiting, uncertain whether to trust Elizabeth or to pursue his projects on the Netherlands. In the end of the year a decision had to be made, as Alençon was offered the sovereignty of the Netherlands, which he accepted. Elizabeth professed to see that he could not do otherwise; she promised to help him with money, and wrote a letter which revived his hopes. "I will ask of God," she said, "this sole grace, that He may crown all the work in such way that Monsieur may have no reason on my part to repent of his election. I firmly believe that my happiness will be too great for an old woman, for whom Paternosters are more fitting than marriage festivities. Nevertheless I shall be always ready to receive commissioners when it shall please you to send them."

So, in the beginning of 1581, the marriage was again up in all seriousness on the side of France. Alençon sent his secretary to inquire if the commissioners to arrange the marriage treaty might safely be sent. Elizabeth was all eagerness; and the secretary returned charged with a letter and a ring for the lucky lover. Elizabeth had no time for business of State, but was apparently engrossed in arranging for the reception of the French Commissioners. Her talk was of tournaments and balls; her one desire was that the fairest ladies in England should grace her Court. The Lords were bidden to bring their families to London, that there might be the bustle of constant gaiety. A large banqueting hall was erected in the palace of Westminster, at which four hundred workmen laboured for a month. New carriages were designed for the use of the Court. The merchants were ordered to sell their silks, velvets and cloth of gold at a reduction of a quarter of the ordinary price, that more should be induced to buy, and so enhance the general splendour.

There was no longer any popular discontent at the idea of the marriage. If the Queen chose to have it so, no more was to be said. Sidney, who had so strongly protested the year before, now lent his aid to entertain the ambassadors of France. He, with the Earl of Arundel, Lord Windsor, and Fulke Greville, devised a diversion after the fashion of the day. Calling themselves the Four Children of Desire, they purposed to capture the Fortress of Perfect Beauty, the abode of Elizabeth, which for this purpose was erected in the tilt-yard at Whitehall. They notified their intent by a defiance, which was delivered to the Queen as she left her chapel, one Sunday morning, by a fantastic messenger. On the appointed day the challengers appeared in splendid array, and, after many songs and speeches, bombarded the Fort of Beauty with flowers, while its cannon replied with volleys of perfumes. Then entered the defenders of the fort, each of whom gave an account of himself and the cause of his coming. Two of them represented Adam and Eve, whose knowledge of the punishment due to presumption led them to defend the beauty of Elizabeth, which shone like the sun and illumined the earth. A mimic fight followed in which the challengers were beaten off. Next day they changed their tactics. Wearied and half-vanquished they came drawn in a car with four horses. Above them was a fair lady who represented Desire. Their eyes were fixed on her, and they sadly confessed that though hope was gone they could not escape her sway. However, they did their best, and the fight waxed furious, till at sunset a herald was sent to the Queen to declare the submission of the challengers. They had learned that Desire could not capture a fortress which was defended by Virtue.

Of such like entertainments the French ambassadors had enough; but when they came to business Elizabeth hesitated. She asked for letters from Alençon; when they arrived she raised political difficulties; would the French King help his brother in the Low Countries? The answer came with unexpected promptness that not only would the King do so, but would make a league with England, offensive and defensive, on any reasonable terms. Elizabeth felt that the toils were gathering round her, and began to look anxiously for an escape. Again a marriage treaty was drawn up, which only required the personal ratification of Elizabeth and Alençon. No sooner had the ambassadors gone than Elizabeth sent to ask for further explanations. The French King was only too accommodating. Elizabeth was at her wit's end, and finally sent Walsingham with a pathetic message. She loved Alençon and would marry him in time; but she could not marry him while marriage would expose her country to a war; she could not ask him to desert the Netherlands: she would, therefore, give him secret help, and wait for her marriage till more peaceful times. Walsingham could only report that if the Queen would not keep her promise, she must be prepared to pay; a substantial sum of money might still induce France to make a political league. This message affected Elizabeth in a vital point. She sobbed and declared that every one had betrayed her. She had always suspected that Alençon only wooed her money; now she had certain proof. But there was no escape. Even a Queen had to pay the penalty for breach of promise of marriage; and two hundred thousand crowns had to be given for a renewal of the league with France. Elizabeth was afraid lest she might be asked for more, and professed a willingness to sacrifice her person to save her purse.

Again Alençon was tempted from his post in the Netherlands, and, against the will of his brother, came to England in the beginning of November, 1581. The Queen received him with every appearance of cordiality, and discussed with him everything except the day for their marriage. An envoy was sent from the French Court to ask for a definite answer. When he arrived he found Alençon and Elizabeth walking in the gallery at Greenwich. She heard his message and answered: "Write to your master that the Duke will be my husband". Then she turned and kissed Alençon, drew a ring from her finger and placed it upon his. She summoned her household and presented Alençon as their future master. Everything seemed settled; but when Hatton came in tears to bewail his own fate, she told him that she meant to ask more than the French King would grant. "But if he does," said

Hatton, "how will you escape?" "With words," she answered, "the current coin in France. Moreover, when the field is large, and the soldiers cowardly, there are always ways for creeping out." In pursuance of this policy she demanded the dissolution of the Seminary of Rheims, the abolition of the Scottish League, and the restitution of Calais. She knew that this last demand was impossible; yet Alençon would not leave England. She pointed out the need of his presence in the Netherlands and promised him money; he said that he had her plighted word, her letters, and her ring, and he must stay till he had her for his wife. Burghley tried without avail to persuade him to go. Even the intimation that, if he stayed till New Year's Day, he would have to give the Queen a costly present did not shake the resolution of the French adventurer. Then Elizabeth declared that she could not marry one who differed from her in religion: Alençon was ready for love of her to adopt her creed. She proposed that she should be his friend, his sister: he pleaded that he suffered untold anguish for her sake, and would rather they both should die than leave England till she was his. Elizabeth exclaimed in agitation that "he must not threaten a poor old woman in her own kingdom. Passion, not reason, spoke in him, or she would think him mad. He must not use such dreadful words." "No, madam," protested Alençon, "you mistake my meaning. I would not hurt your blessed person. I meant that I would rather be cut in pieces than not marry you, and so be laughed at by the world." So saying he burst into tears; whereupon Elizabeth kindly lent him her handkerchief that he might wipe his eyes. Never was a more ludicrously bewildering situation. At last, in February, 1582, Alençon was with difficulty hustled out of the country, on the plea that his presence was sorely needed in the Netherlands. The Queen went with him to Canterbury, still protesting her sorrow at his departure, and wishing for the dawn of happier days when she might safely fulfil her promise: meanwhile he was to write to her as his wife. Alençon was safely conveyed to Flushing; and no sooner was he gone than Elizabeth declared that she would give a million that her "dear

Frog should again be swimming in the Thames, and not in the marshes of the Low Countries".

Politics never sunk to a lower level of absurdity than in these ridiculous proceedings. We are tempted to credit Elizabeth with a deliberate intention of exposing the folly of the prevalent system of regulating national interests by Royal marriages. Doubtless she saw, early in her career, what her advisers did not see with equal clearness, that no marriage would really help her or England. She played with proposals at first to content her advisers and her people. When she had reached a point at which no one thought her marriage would be desirable, she punished their previous short-sightedness by taking up a proposal of marriage on her own account. In early years her affections might be involved, and her sense of personal dignity outraged by the suggestions which were constantly submitted to her; and she rebelled as a woman at the idea of self-sacrifice for an uncertain good. As she grew older such feelings passed away, and she was sure of herself. She took a perverse pleasure in bewildering her ministers and her favourites; she seized an opportunity of reading them a lesson. Moreover, by so doing, she took affairs of State out of their hands at a time when it was difficult to determine on any course of action. She was resolved for once to make her personal influence felt throughout Europe, and for two years she kept political action waiting on the declaration of her pleasure. She was pressed for a decision on many matters. She saw no decision which could be wisely made. So she resolved to keep things as they were by embarking unaided on an adventure of which she did not in the least foresee the end. She trusted to her own dexterity; and when things went further than she expected she did not scruple about her dignity, but sacrificed it without hesitation. After all, the episode of the Alençon marriage is only the policy of Elizabeth, writ large in a particular instance. She was ready to do anything in order to avert any definite misfortune that was impending. If only the present was saved, there was hope for the future. She had no confidence in great schemes, but preferred to grow strong by little gains carefully secured. So she balanced France against Spain, without allowing either to win from the other. She saw that a desire to get rid of Alençon from France was a motive of French interference in the Netherlands. She played with Alençon as a cat plays with a mouse, and was ready to catch him in her claws again whenever he showed signs of vitality. At the bottom of all this lay a desire to know if Alençon would really succeed, if France would really join with England against Spain. Perhaps Elizabeth was not entirely insincere in her regrets for Alençon's departure. Had he been a greater man her attitude might have been different. When she is blamed for want of boldness, for not joining France in expelling Spain from the Netherlands, it must be remembered that success depended on the character of the French leader. Elizabeth saw and judged for herself. She was wise in hesitating to trust her fortunes to the man she saw. Yet, when he went away from England, Elizabeth probably meant that, if he gave her an assurance of his success, she was still ready to become his wife. It is true that by this hesitation much was lost. Alençon went to the Netherlands discredited, and soon showed himself a mere adventurer. He tried to seize for himself the towns which he had come to defend, and was driven ignominiously in flight from Antwerp. He died in May, 1585, and Elizabeth played her part to the end. "The Queen," wrote the French ambassador, "is in appearance full of tears and regrets, telling me that she is a widow who has lost her husband, and how I know that the late Monsieur was much to her, and how she ever held him hers, although they had not lived together, and many other such speeches; for she is a Princess who knows how to compose and transform herself as suits her best."

We fail, however, to understand the full bearing of Elizabeth's conduct to Alençon if we do not keep in mind the perils by which she was beset. The time of tranquillity which England had been enjoying came abruptly to an end in 1580, and Elizabeth's throne was once more insecure. Besides the forces of France and Spain there were other forces at work which were more difficult to keep in check, the forces of the Roman Catholic reaction. The excommunication of Elizabeth had been intended by the Pope as a declaration of war against England. It was an assertion that all European States must owe allegiance to him, and that those which refused to recognise his supremacy must be reduced to obedience in the common interest of all. The great question decided in the sixteenth century was that States might exist without submitting to the Papal jurisdiction; and England was the country on which the fate of Protestantism depended. If England could be reduced, all other rebels might be won back; and the Pope was anxious to impress this truth on his allies. But France and Spain had their own interest to pursue, and their own reasons for keeping on good terms with England for a time. The day would come when Elizabeth would be dethroned; but the immediate season was not convenient.

Meanwhile the band of English Romanists who had left England after Elizabeth's accession waited in vain. They had fled in the hopes of a speedy return. They carried with them the picture of England as it had been in Mary's days, and were unable to understand the change which had slowly passed over the popular mind since then. To them Elizabeth was a usurper and a tyrant. The only accounts which reached them were sent by the intriguers who gathered round Mary Queen of Scots. They were singularly out of sympathy with the main current of English feeling, and they unconsciously misrepresented it abroad. Their writings and their statements did much to create prejudices which have scarcely yet been removed. In the light of subsequent events nothing can seem more ignoble than the restless intrigues of this band of misguided schemers. We have to remind ourselves that they were striving for a political ideal which was not yet entirely condemned by events. They laboured to keep alive in England the elements of disaffection which they believed, with a little help from outside, would soon gather an overwhelming force. It is the great merit of Elizabeth that she was keenly aware that their efforts could only be withstood by the growth of a national

spirit, slowly created by an appreciation of the benefits conferred
by her government. It might seem wise to precipitate a crisis, and
press for a decision; but she was of opinion that the gradual con-
solidation of her people into a new sense of national life was the
only safe course to pursue. When danger came it must not be of
her seeking. Her people must feel that the menace was to themselves in the first place, and only to the Queen as their representative.

So Elizabeth waited to be attacked, and spared no pains to
defer the time of the attack, which she always felt to be
imminent. Her cautious policy exasperated her opponents, who
wearied of waiting for action on the part of the King of Spain.
At last they resolved to take action by themselves; if they succeeded, help would soon be forthcoming. In 1580 a plan was
formed, with the Pope's sanction, for attacking England in three
directions, first through Ireland, secondly through Scotland, and
thirdly by raising disaffection in England itself. This was to be
done cautiously and secretly; but all the three advances were to
be made at the same time.

(1) Ireland was a great difficulty to Elizabeth's government.
It was necessary to guard it lest it should be used as a point of
attack, but as little money must be spent on it as possible. Henry
VIII. had endeavoured to civilise the Irish people through their
chiefs, who were to be converted from tribal chieftains to feudal
nobles. This policy might have succeeded but for the breach with
the Papacy, for which the Irish were not prepared, not feeling
the same grievances. The changes made in England were forced
upon Ireland without being explained; and disaffection was the
natural result. At the beginning of her reign Elizabeth had to face
trouble in Ireland, arising from the difference between Irish and
English law. Henry VIII. had created Con O'Neill Earl of
Tyrone, and civil jurisdiction went with the earldom. On his
death, in 1559, his illegitimate son claimed to succeed him, and
was elected as the O'Neill, to the exclusion of his nephew, who
was regarded as the rightful heir by English law. Shan O'Neill

made good his position, and even defeated the Lord-Deputy, the Earl of Sussex. He came to London to plead his cause, and Elizabeth was fain to conciliate him; but on his return Shan went his own way and defied all the efforts of Sussex. It was not till 1567 that he was at length put down by Sir Henry Sidney, after causing Elizabeth an expenditure of nearly £500,000. He had succeeded, however, in checking the hope of Anglicising the Irish, by raising the old tribal chieftainship to importance, and in pointing out that England was saddled with a dependency which would welcome an invader, and would rise at the summons of the Pope. "They all look to Spain," wrote a Spaniard, "to deliver them from English tyranny, to save their souls, and give them back the blessed Mass."

After Elizabeth's excommunication an offer of the sovereignty of Ireland was made by some of the Irish to Philip of Spain, and there was talk of a Spanish invasion. This only increased the ill-will between the English and the Irish, and a simmering rebellion was kept down by much barbarity. Sidney ruined himself in trying to keep order; and his successor, Sir William Fitzwilliam, fared no better. Attempts were made to colonise parts of Ireland from England. In 1573 Walter Devereux, newly created Earl of Essex, set out to occupy a large portion of Ulster. Though he went resolved "to win the Irish by kindness," his undertaking ended in disastrous failure. He sacrificed his money and stained his fair fame by treacherous deeds. In 1576 he died hopeless of the future. Ireland had already become the grave of English reputations.

Briefly, the condition of affairs in Ireland was this. The Irish people were sacrificed to the conflict which was raging in Europe, and their interests were considered neither by the English Government nor by the Romanist plotters. The latter stirred them to rebellion by promises of Spanish help which never came; the former regarded them with suspicion and kept them down by barbarities. It was a grave misfortune that England, engaged in a serious conflict for its existence, could only regard Ireland as its most vulnerable point. Elizabeth could not afford to spend money on its reduction, and her policy of doing always the least possible was there especially disastrous. Deputies were sent against their will to a hopeless task. They were ill-furnished with supplies, and attempted to enforce their power by isolated acts of violence, which only intensified the existing ill-will. Moreover, the extension of English influence was resisted because it carried with it a religious change which was distasteful; and Irish national sentiment gathered round adhesion to the Papacy.

This state of things seemed promising to the Romanist cause. One of the most active of the English refugees, Nicholas Sanders, combined with a brother of the Earl of Desmond, James Fitzmorris, to raise Ireland in the Pope's name. Invested with the office of legate, and trusting to the influence of the name of Fitzmorris, he landed in Kerry with a few Spanish troops in July, 1579, and built a fort at Smerwick, on Dingle Bay. The news caused great stir in Ireland, and much alarm in England. Elizabeth complained to the Spanish ambassador, and received answer that the Spaniards had not been sent by the King. There were few English troops in Ireland; and when Fitzmorris was killed in the first encounter Elizabeth treated the invasion as of no consequence. She was economical, as usual, and countermanded the supplies which she had ordered in the first panic. But the Earl of Desmond joined the rebels, and Ireland was in a dangerous state. Lord Grey de Wilton was sent as deputy from England; and at the same time the Pope sent a reinforcement of eight hundred men, Italians and Spaniards, who entrenched themselves in the fort of Smerwick. An English fleet was sent to attack the fort by sea, while Grey gathered such forces as he could by land. Amongst those who served under him were Walter Raleigh and Edmund Spenser. After two days' bombardment the fort surrendered on November 9, 1580. Lord Grey asked the garrison if they had any commission from their King to wage war in Ireland. The Italians answered that they were sent by the Pope for the defence of the Catholic faith. Grey replied that the Pope had no authority from God or man, and was not their natural prince; he could only look on them as pirates. They pressed to be admitted to terms, but Grey absolutely refused. They were driven to surrender at discretion, and six hundred of them were shot. It was a terrible warning, and Elizabeth seems to have felt no remorse. At all events she wrote to Grey, with her own hand, a characteristic note: "The mighty hand of the Almightiest power hath showed manifest by the force of His strength in the weakness of feeblest sex and mind this year, to make men ashamed ever afterwards to disdain us. In which action I joy that you have been chosen the instrument of His glory, which I mean to give you no cause to forthink."

The end of the Papal attempt on Ireland was disappointment to those who planned it, and misery to the people. Sanders perished wretchedly in a bog. The Earl of Desmond was harried from place to place till he was slain. Large tracts of the country became desert. The unhappy Irish had been lured to rebellion by hopes of help, which they did not entirely trust, but which they could not refuse to entertain. The only result was to convince England that Romanism and disloyalty were the same, and to widen the breach between the English and the Irish peoples.

(2) The attempt on Scotland was made in a more subtle and insidious way. Esmé Stuart, nephew and heir of the Earl of Lennox, and therefore closely related to the Scottish King, had been educated in France, and was an accomplished and captivating gentleman. It was natural that he should return to his native land; and it was equally natural that, with his gifts of manner, he should at the age of twenty-three be more acceptable to a boy of fourteen than the somewhat grim advisers by whom he had hitherto been surrounded. So Esmé Stuart went to Scotland in September, 1579, the secret agent of the Pope and the Duke of Guise, commissioned to bring back Scotland to its old alliance with France, and to its allegiance to the Papacy. But Stuart was willing to dissemble his religious convictions, and hide his political plans under an appearance of careless geniality. He soon won

the King's favour, and was created Earl, and afterwards Duke, of Lennox. He saw that the first thing to be done was the removal of the Earl of Morton, who was the actual governor of Scotland, and in favour of the English alliance. Morton foresaw his danger and asked help from Elizabeth, who showed her usual hesitation to commit herself. Lennox used his opportunity; Morton was seized and charged with complicity in Darnley's murder. When Elizabeth thought of coming to his help, she was disarmed by a public profession of Protestantism made by Lennox. Morton was executed in June, 1581; Lennox was master of Scotland, and the English party was practically destroyed. Jesuits were at once dispatched to effect the conversion of the young King, who had suffered too much from the rigorous discipline of the Presbyterian clergy to have much affection for them. The next step in this scheme was the restoration of the French alliance. But here arose a technical difficulty. James had not been recognised by France as King of Scotland; and Mary demanded that she should be associated with him in the kingdom by an Act of the Scottish Parliament.

Before the King could be converted, or Mary's punctiliousness relieved, the Scots took alarm on religious grounds, and resisted an attempt to elect a new bishop to the vacant See of Glasgow. Round this religious resistance the English party was slowly formed again, and was secretly supported by Elizabeth. The result was, in August, 1582, the Earl of Gowrie and some confederate nobles seized the King as he was on his way to a hunting expedition, and carried him off to Gowrie House. Lennox had not the courage to face such a crisis. Afraid for his personal safety, he left Scotland in December, and died in Paris in May, 1583. It was now in Elizabeth's power to make an agreement with James; but this she refused to do. It was sufficient for her that, with Mary in her hands, she could hold the mother against the son. She had learned the difficulties in the way of associating James and Mary. She knew that James had need of her, and was afraid of his mother. So she refused to make a treaty which would have involved a payment on her part. "Her servants and favourites," she said, "professed to love her for her high qualities; Alençon for her beauty; and the Scots for her crown. But all came to the same in the end. They wanted nothing but her money, and they should not have it."

The result of the Roman invasion of Scotland was a complete failure. It only strengthened Scottish Protestantism, and showed the young King his true position and his hopes for the future.

(3) The third detachment of the Papal invaders had, meanwhile, landed in England itself. One object of the English refugees was to bring those in England who professed the old form of religion into line with the principles of the Romanist revival. If Elizabeth had not been excommunicated, they might have been allowed to continue their own worship in private, and their loyalty would not have been called in question. There would have grown up a tacit recognition of their position within limits which might have gradually expanded. But the excommunication of Elizabeth was an open declaration of war, and exposed the loyalty of the English Romanists to perpetual suspicion. Those who wished to be loyal were not permitted to remain so, but were surrounded by intrigues from which they could not escape. Elizabeth's rule, they were told, was unlawful and would be only temporary; they must be prepared to use any opportunity for bringing it to an end. This being so, the most fervent amongst them preferred to leave England and openly work for their avowed end. The seminary at Rheims invited young men to be educated in the true principles of activity for the Papal restoration. A new body of priests came into existence, unlike the old priests, who merely remained constant to the system in which they had been brought up. Their successors were men trained in a foreign system, and animated—it might be unconsciously—with a spirit which regarded the subjugation of England to Rome as the first and foremost object of their endeavour. Such enthusiasts were naturally drawn to the rigid organisation of the Society of

Jesus, and the Jesuits undertook to revive the drooping spirits of the English Romanists by a mission.

The object of supplying religious ministrations to such as desired them is one which must command our sympathies, especially when it was carried out in the face of serious danger. But it was the misfortune of the Papal policy that it had made it impossible to separate the spiritual from the political object of such a mission. It is true that Pope Gregory XIII. did something to make it wear a religious character. He issued an explanation of the Bull of excommunication, stating that it was always binding on the Queen and her adherents, but not upon Catholics as things stood; that is, that the Queen and her Government were bound to consider themselves excommunicated, but Catholics need not regard them so as long as they continued in power. The effect of this was to make it lawful for the Romanists to obey the government of their country, so long as it existed; but it was left uncertain what steps they were justified in taking to change it. It only meant that they were to profess loyalty until Elizabeth could safely be attacked; then they were to join her foes. Moreover, there remained the question: If the Romanists could without mortal sin conspire against the life of Elizabeth. It is sadly certain that, six months after the issue of the explanatory brief, the Papal nuncio in Spain gave his opinion that the Bull of Pius V. justified all her subjects in taking arms against the Queen; as regards her assassination, the Pope would not make any declaration previously, but would give the necessary absolutions after the deed had been done. Further, the Jesuit mission landed in England at the same time that the Pope was sending troops to Ireland. It was too much to expect that the Pope should be understood to be acting in his temporal capacity in one case, and in his spiritual capacity in another.

Elizabeth was aware of what was intended, and prepared for it by ordering the laws against the Romanists to be more strictly enforced. She also ordered all who had sons or relations abroad to call them home, and declared that all who harboured Jesuits would be regarded as maintainers of rebels. She further issued a proclamation to her people, proudly claiming that never had justice been better administered, and never had a country enjoyed greater peace than England under her rule. Had it not been for a few traitors, the record of peace would have been unbroken. Now that a new disturbance was projected, she must use her power to keep her land free alike "from the bondage of the Romish tyranny" and from foreign invasion; for this purpose she trusted to the good will and courage of her people. It is in such utterances as these that we find the key to Elizabeth's policy. She wished to be able to lay before her people definite results of which all might judge, not a record of great attempts which had burdened the country and produced nothing that could be appraised. Every year of peace, every tax avoided, was so much that swelled her claim upon her people's gratitude; and her one care was that this should steadily increase.

The leaders of the first Jesuit mission, Parsons and Campion, landed in England in June, 1580. They were chosen to represent the two-fold aspect of the Papal policy; Parsons was a political intriguer, Campion a simple-minded religious enthusiast. An association of young men of good families was formed for their protection, and clad in various disguises they were rapidly passed on from place to place. Campion was a man of attractive character, and convincing eloquence. His high qualities gained in power from the romantic charm which was attached to his adventure. There was, at first, no organisation of police which was sufficient to baffle him. His services were attended by throngs; and several noblemen were reconciled to the Roman Church, among them the brother and the son of the late Duke of Norfolk, Lord Henry Howard and the Earl of Arundel. There was general alarm, during which Parliament met in January, 1581, and passed an "Act to Restrain Her Majesty's Subjects in their due Allegiance," which made it high treason to reconcile any to the Church of Rome, or to aid or conceal those who were so doing. It was forbidden, under heavy fines, to say Mass, or to refuse attendance at the service of the Established Church. Another Act made it felony to publish any libel against the Queen.

This legislation was a serious deviation from the policy which had hitherto been pursued about ecclesiastical matters. At the beginning of the reign an Act of Uniformity had set up a religious system which, it was hoped, would slowly absorb all different opinions, and be in time universally accepted. The excommunication of Elizabeth had made it politically necessary to cut off intercourse with Rome. Now the Roman invasion had led to the adoption of repression on grounds of national expediency. This reacted disastrously upon the position of the English Church, which was arrested in its development by being imposed as a test, not of religious conviction, but of patriotism. It was felt by many that this was not a position which could be justified. Compulsory attendance at Church services was as distasteful to the advanced Puritans as it was to the Romanists, and drove them to separate into distinct bodies as a protest. Their loyalty was not doubted, and they were consequently seldom visited with penalties, to which the Romanists were habitually exposed. This gave the action of the government an appearance of unfairness, while it involved the Church in the charge of persecution. It is easier to point out the evils of the course adopted than to suggest a remedy. The action of the Pope had made it almost impossible to distinguish between his spiritual and his temporal claims. It was hard for the government to observe a distinction which he had ingeniously contrived to abolish in practice, while professing a wish to maintain it in theory.

The Jesuits, elated at their first success, continued their efforts with increasing boldness. In June appeared a book written by Campion, *Ten Reasons for being a Catholic*, of which copies were found laid in the seats of St. Mary's Church at Oxford. This audacity made efforts to capture him more zealous, and finally he was taken after a rigorous search among the hiding places devised in the solid walls of the manor house at Lydford, near Abingdon. He was brought to London in his disguise as a layman, with a placard on his head, "Campion, the seditious Jesuit". Yet Elizabeth was anxious to deal mercifully with him. He was secretly conveyed to the house of the Earl of Leicester, where Elizabeth was present. She asked if he acknowledged her as Queen, and he said yes. She asked if he thought the Pope might lawfully excommunicate her. He answered that he could not judge in so high a controversy, wherein the greatest divines were not agreed. He must follow Christ's example and answer the dilemma that he would pay Her Majesty what was hers, and to God what was His. Campion was doubtless sincere in thinking that this answer was enough: but its general meaning was that he claimed the advantage of a divided allegiance; he would obey the Queen when it suited him to do so, and would reserve obedience to the Pope's temporal commands till it was safe or expedient.

The procedure by torture was applied to Campion and other captured priests. It is horrible to read how they were racked and questioned to discover their accomplices. The object of the government was to treat them as traitors, to separate their political from their religious mission. It was the object of the priests to declare that they had not meddled with politics, but had confined themselves to religious teaching. Their confessions under torture were all so construed as to implicate them in treasonable practices; and, in November, Campion and fourteen others were brought to trial on the charge of having conspired against the Queen by attempting to raise sedition in England and to bring on a foreign invasion. Campion, broken by the rack, and unable to move his arms, conducted his defence with great ability. No treason had been proved against him; he was accused solely for his religion. "What force excommunications be of, what authority is due to the Bishop of Rome, how men's consciences must be instructed, are no matters of fact, nor triable by jurors, but points yet disputed and not yet resolved in the schools." He claimed the right to suspend his judgment on such points. But all was in vain; it was not the single-minded enthusiast who was on trial, but the aggressive system behind him, of which he was the unconscious instrument. He was condemned to a traitor's death, and, with two companions, was hanged on December 1, 1581. He died saying: "I will and do pray for the Queen". "For which Queen?" he was asked. "For Elizabeth," was the answer, "your Queen and mine, to whom I wish a long quiet reign and all prosperity."

Men felt there was something amiss in such a death of such a man; but they drew different conclusions. Some were drawn to admiration of those who could die so calmly for what they held to be true. One young Norfolk gentleman who was standing by, Henry Walpole, was converted to Romanism because a drop of Campion's blood, as he was being quartered, spurted upon his clothes. He was carried away by the horror of the scene, and the sympathy of the bystanders. The majority of Englishmen ground their teeth in anger that the Pope should send such men to do his work of alternately cajoling and coercing England into the abandonment of its new-won freedom. They saw through the cruel dilemma, which he had so skilfully constructed, and associated Rome and Roman methods with trickery and deceit. The English mind was never given to draw fine distinctions and disliked to be bewildered. Adhesion to the Papacy became synonymous with prevarication, underhand dealing, and a disregard for truth. That England should separate from the Roman Church was one thing; the terms and the results of the separation were another. The papal policy sowed the seeds of misunderstanding and mutual dislike, which went on growing. It created the impression that Romanism was not only anti-English in its political aims, but un-English in its methods and in its contents.

Moreover, the Romanists had some justification for representing England as adopting their own methods. The story of the English martyrs was spread over the Continent and seemed a repetition of the cruelties of the Inquisition. Pamphlets relating the cruelty of Elizabeth were cried in the streets. Burghley attempted to answer the outcry by a book, *The Execution of Jus-*

tice in England, not for Religion, but for Treason. Allen answered by a *Defence of the English Catholics,* which was better adapted for foreign consumption. England was misrepresented and misunderstood abroad, and its separation from Continental influences became more complete.

The Papal attempt on England through the Jesuit mission failed as the other attempts had failed; but it left an evil mark behind. The Papal claims confounded religion and politics, things spiritual and things temporal. England in repelling these claims was driven to use methods, and adopt a position, which perilously resembled those of the system against which it strove.

VI

THE CRISIS

৵§ That her realm might discover its own capacities, Elizabeth had nurtured it in peace. England used its opportunity by developing industrial life on one hand, and a spirit of naval adventure on the other. It was the simultaneous growth in these two directions which formed a new England. From the first Elizabeth had favoured the maritime spirit, and had made use of it to hinder the advance of Spain in the Netherlands. But it was clear that the strength of Spain lay in the gold of the New World and Englishmen were eager to traffic in the Western Seas. The disastrous voyage of Hawkins only inspired with a desire for revenge a young kinsman of his, Francis Drake, who, in 1572, captured a convoy of bullion at Panama, and on seeing the South Pacific from the mountains, "fell on his knees and prayed God that he might one day navigate those waters". To Drake it was intolerable that Spain should claim a monopoly of the commerce of half the world, and he was prepared to resist the claim to the utmost. There was some difficulty in discovering a method of doing it, as England was at peace with Spain. But Englishmen in that day were not troubled by scruples; they were ready to undertake responsibility on their own account, to act first, and to find justification for their action afterwards. Elizabeth was willing to give secret help, without compromising herself openly, on the understanding that she was at liberty to disavow all complicity if it suited her to do so. Drake was prepared to put to sea, knowing that he ran the risk of being hanged as a pirate, but that he also had a chance of being hailed as a national hero.

At the end of 1577, when the relations between England and

Spain were uncertain, Drake sailed from Plymouth with five small vessels, fitted out by a few adventurers, amongst whom the Queen and the Earl of Leicester were the largest shareholders. His nominal object was to explore the unknown parts of the Pacific; his real object was to teach Philip that he was not secure in the part of the world which he considered most exclusively his own. The story of his adventurous voyage need not be told here. He was the first Englishman who passed through the Straits of Magellan, and he used to the full the advantage of being an unexpected visitor. He seized the stores of bullion which were ready for shipment to Spain, and captured a treasure-ship which was richly laden. In August, 1579, Philip heard the news of his losses. His ambassador expostulated, and a breach with Spain seemed imminent. But, just at this time, Philip was preparing to claim the crown of Portugal and did not wish to quarrel with England. Elizabeth tried her "gipsy tricks" to wheedle out of the Spanish ambassador whether Portugal or England was first to be attacked. Her attitude was finally determined by the return, in October, 1580, of Drake, after sailing round the globe in his adventurous expedition, which had lasted for three years.

England rang with admiration of his exploits. Elizabeth was delighted at the greatness of his prize, which amounted to nearly £750,000. She was determined not to part with the money, and Hatton gave it as his opinion that, though Drake might have been dealt with as the Spaniards pleased, if they had caught him, there was no legal obligation on the Queen to pay any attention to their complaints against him. So Elizabeth received Drake with honour, and sent orders that his ship, the *Golden Hind*, should be brought up the Thames to Deptford and there preserved. She was entertained at a banquet on board, and dubbed Drake a knight. Meanwhile she took all necessary precautions about the money which he had brought. Following the precedent set in the case of the gold seized twelve years before, she ordered it to be removed to the Tower for safe custody. But she gave orders to the officer, whose duty it was to weigh it, that he should first allow Drake to remove £10,000 for himself, and as much as was necessary to give herself a good return for her outlay. Then the inventory of the rest was sent to the Spanish ambassador. Ultimately she paid her partners in the adventure 100 per cent. and kept the remainder.

She soon had an opportunity of increasing her treasures at Philip's expense. Philip had succeeded to the crown of Portugal, and made good his claims against the pretender, Don Antonio, who came to England, carrying with him the crown jewels, which he sold to the Queen that he might fit out in England an expedition against the Azores. The Spanish ambassador remonstrated and detailed all Philip's grievances—the plunder of Spanish ships, the piratical expedition of Drake, the interference in the Netherlands, and now, the support given to Don Antonio. Elizabeth answered that if she chose to help Don Antonio she could do so to some effect; as to the other matters, she did not know what he meant. Nettled by this insolent tone, Mendoza replied: "If your Majesty will not hear words, we must come to the cannon and see if you will hear them!" Without raising her voice, Elizabeth quietly said: "If you use threats of that kind I will fling you into prison". Then she called her lords in attendance and repeated what Mendoza had said, adding "I told him he need not think to frighten me". The Spaniard replied: "I am not so foolish. Princes do not endure to be threatened by private persons. The Queen, being a lady, and so beautiful a lady, may throw me to the lions if she will." Elizabeth's face cleared at the compliment ("so absurd is she," is Mendoza's comment), and the conversation continued. She would make no restitution of Drake's pillage till Philip had given her satisfaction for his interference in Ireland. As she left the room she muttered with a sigh: "Would to God that each had his own and was at peace".

Philip was not yet prepared to make war on England, and this affair blew over. There were other plans in hand for dealing with the heretical Queen. The part of the Roman scheme which had the greatest hopes of success was the attempt on Scotland, where, if things had gone well, the Duke of Guise was to have landed to assist Lennox. Now that the departure of Lennox had rendered that impossible, why should not Guise land in England, where, the Romanist refugees assured him, everything was ripe for a rebellion? There was the old suggestion that everything could be done much more expediently if Elizabeth were only out of the way. This was so constantly on the lips of the scheming politicians among the Romanist priests that a young country gentleman in Warwickshire, John Somerville, caught fire at the suggestion and went up to London to kill the Queen in October, 1583. He betrayed himself by idle speeches, was put in the Tower and confessed under the rack.

This was an individual attempt. But there was being hatched at the same time a more serious conspiracy by those who were in the secret of Guise's proposed invasion. Francis Throgmorton belonged to a Cheshire family which favoured Mary Stuart. He flitted between London and the Continent, carrying messages from Mary and Mendoza. He was observed leaving Mendoza's house, was watched, and seized as he was writing a letter in cipher. His papers contained a list of the English allies of Guise, and he confessed that Mendoza was to communicate with such Roman Catholics as were justices of the peace, who were to raise levies when the Duke of Guise arrived, under pretence of helping the Queen, and then to use them against her.

The discovery of this plot filled Elizabeth with alarm, and measures of precaution were at once taken. The Earls of Arundel and Northumberland were sent to the Tower. Suspected persons were everywhere imprisoned. The fleet guarded the coast. Levies were called out, and their officers carefully reviewed. Suspected magistrates were removed. A new search was made for Jesuits and seminary priests. The Spanish ambassador was ordered to leave England. Never had things looked worse than at the beginning of the year 1584. Nor did the darkness lighten as the year passed on. First the death of the Duke of Alençon, in May, removed all prospect that France would further interfere to help the Netherlands against Spain. It also brought France itself to the verge of a religious war; for Henry III. was sickly, and the next heir, Henry, King of Navarre, was a Huguenot. The prospect of his accession marshalled France into two opposing factions, and increased the power of the Guises. Next, in July, came the news of the assassination of the Prince of Orange, which left the United Provinces without a leader. Already the Prince of Parma had succeeded in reducing many towns, and his success seemed almost assured. When the Netherlands had been conquered, the Spanish arms would be directed against England, as had always been the intention of Philip. Moreover, Spain had made good its annexation of Portugal, and so had become absolute master of the New World. The Spanish monarchy seemed at the height of its power.

England felt the imminence of the danger, and considered first the most immediate peril, that of the Queen's assassination. It was clear that Elizabeth was the object of ceaseless plots, one of which might at any moment prove successful. She was singularly easy of access and heedless of danger. She refused to take exceptional precautions, saying that she would not be put into custody. Her courage was remarkable, and she did not allow anxiety to weigh upon her. It is curious that her intrepidity served to some degree as a protection. One conspirator, at least, confessed that his intention to kill the Queen failed when he came into her presence and saw her fearless bearing. It is significant of Elizabeth's temper that she deliberately chose to live among her people and commit to them the care of her person. She would not submit to live in guarded seclusion, but made her influence felt as a living presence.

But though Elizabeth did not fear, it was otherwise with her ministers. The death of the Queen meant immediate anarchy, the probable accession of Mary Queen of Scots, and the overthrow of everything which they had accomplished. Elizabeth's responsibility ceased at her death; but those left behind must devise some means for their own protection. They wished to have some assurance about the future. Elizabeth always baffled them. She would have no future; they must depend on her alone. In course of time men grew accustomed to this position; but when the murder of the Prince of Orange showed them what might occur in England, they were filled with alarm. The murder of the Queen would put an end to all authority. No one had power to act, and the question of succession could not be settled without civil war. The Council discussed how some basis of action might be constructed, some practical steps suggested, which might hold the country together for a time. They devised a proposal for a voluntary bond of association, expressing a policy which those who signed it pledged themselves to carry out. By this means, at all events, a strong national party would be formed, with definite intentions of which it had given formal notice to Europe.

The bond of association was for the protection of the person of Elizabeth. It set forth that "for the furtherance and advancement of some pretended title to the Crown, the life of our sovereign has been most dangerously designed against". The signatories therefore bound themselves to defend Elizabeth "against all States, dignities and earthly powers whatever". They would withstand to the utmost all who acted, counselled, or consented to the harm of the Queen's person. Should any attempt against her succeed, they would not accept as her successor any one "by whom, or for whom, any such detestable act shall be attempted or committed, as unworthy of all government in any Christian realm or State"; further, they would "prosecute such persons to the death". This document was first signed in London and Middlesex, and then was sent round the other counties. Everywhere it was signed with enthusiasm. Indeed no one of any importance could have ventured to withhold his signature.

The meaning of this document was a menace to Mary Queen of Scots and her adherents at home and abroad. They were warned that if their plots of assassination succeeded, or if a foreign invasion were made in her name, the immediate result would be that she would be put to death. Whatever else happened, she, at all events, would not follow Elizabeth on the English throne. To make this warning more intelligible, Mary was removed from the care of Lord Shrewsbury, where she had been treated as an honoured guest, and was placed in the safe keeping, first of Sir Ralph Sadler, and afterwards of Sir Amyas Paulet, both of whom were devoted servants of Elizabeth, and would at once take action in an emergency. For greater security she was placed in the Castle of Tutbury, a fortress rather than a dwelling-house, desolate and uncomfortable, where she was closely guarded and cut off from means of communication with her friends outside.

It was necessary that what had been done spontaneously in the form of a voluntary association should obtain some formal sanction. Parliament was summoned for this purpose in the end of 1584. Burghley drafted a measure for a provisional government, in case of the Queen's death, which should continue till the criminals had been punished and the succession had been decided. Elizabeth, however, was not prepared to go farther than give legal force to the Association, and the Bill which she recommended for this purpose was so insufficient that it was dropped. Ultimately an Act was passed which declared that any one in whose behalf an invasion was made, or a rebellion attempted, or anything devised to the hurt of the Queen's person, should be for ever excluded from the succession. All subjects might, on the Queen's direction, pursue to death any such person. If the attempt succeeded, a Commission was appointed to examine into the cause of the Queen's death and punish all who were concerned in it. Another Act was passed which ordered all Jesuits and seminary priests to quit the realm within forty days; those who were found in England after that time were guilty of high treason, and those who harboured them of felony. Children sent abroad for education were to return to England, otherwise they were incapable of inheriting. No one was to leave the country without the Queen's permission.

When this Bill was introduced, one member, William Parry, opposed it as "bloody, desperate and full of pernicious consequences". The temper of the House would brook no opposition; he was committed to the sergeant-at-arms, placed at the bar, and asked to explain his words. He said that he would only explain to the Queen, and he was taken before the Council. Elizabeth sent a message that she hoped Parry would be forgiven; and he promised not to offend again. But before the House had been dissolved, Parry was accused by an accomplice of having conspired against the Queen's life. Parry was an adventurer, with an indifferent record. He had been one of Burghley's spies, but had become a Roman Catholic, and undertook to kill the Queen. In the course of the summer he had sought interviews with her to give her information about other plots. He admitted that he had intended to take her life, but his courage failed. Parry seems to have been a man of unstable character, bordering on insanity, with no clear idea of what he was doing. But his confession showed that danger was on every side, and he was condemned to death.

The severity of this legislation showed that the country was fully roused, and the Roman Catholic party quailed before it. The Earl of Arundel, who had been restored to favour, attempted to flee from England. He wrote a letter to Elizabeth, in which he said he was exposed to the malice of enemies, and that he retired abroad to escape the fate of his father. He was captured at sea, brought back, and committed to the Tower, where he ended his days. His fellow-conspirator, the Earl of Northumberland, was more deeply implicated in Throgmorton's conspiracy, and, to avoid a trial, shot himself in his prison. The expectations of Elizabeth's domestic foes were vanishing, and they were reduced to despair. They waited, but nothing came. Elizabeth's government grew stronger at home, and they had no hopes of overthrowing it. The country was united in its favour; so those who had been merely waiting accepted it, while those who had committed themselves against it felt that England was no longer safe for them.

Still Elizabeth was left to face the danger that Spain was on the point of stamping out the rebellion in the Netherlands; and this would be a standing danger to England. Elizabeth had reaped great advantages from the revolt, but had steadily declined to identify herself with it. She never expected that it would be ultimately successful; and she knew that, if she openly assisted rebels in another country, she would be setting an example which might be followed in England. So she kept alive the spirits of the Netherlanders from time to time: she gave them assistance when it suited her purposes; she encouraged France to interfere, but was unwilling that France should oust Spain. She wished the revolt to go on as long as possible; she wished the Netherlands at last to make as good terms as possible, and win a large amount of self-government. But she could not afford to see them crushed just at this period. As there was no one else to help them, she must unwillingly do so herself. The states were eager for English help; the party which supported the Prince of Orange saw no one to replace him except Elizabeth, and they offered her the sovereignty.

It was an offer which would have tempted most rulers—an accession of territory and of a people who had long been connected by commercial ties with England, a people of seamen engaged in industry, a people who were striving against oppression for religious liberty. It was a prospect which opened up possibilities of a great policy, the formation of a Protestant League, the establishment of a naval supremacy, the foundation of a colonial empire. Nothing is more characteristic of Elizabeth's statesmanship than that she declined the offer, and was not tempted for a moment to leave the path which she had marked out for herself. She was eager for small gains, but she refused great opportunities. She would not embark on enterprises of which she could not foresee the end. She pursued no great ideals. It was enough for her to foster England's gradual growth; she would not imperil that process by rash adventure. The annexation of the Netherlands meant an endless war with Spain, round which all European questions might gather. It might be that war was inevitable, but there was a wide difference between a war of aggression and a war of defence. She could trust her people to defend their liberties at home; she could not trust them to bear the continued strain of military operations in the Low Countries. It was a serious matter to engage against such a general as Parma, backed by the resources of Spain, which were thought to be greater than they really were. Even if those operations were successful, and the Spaniards were driven out, France would look with no friendly eye on the English as their neighbours, and the possession of the Netherlands would be a permanent difficulty to England.

So Elizabeth seems to have reasoned—whether wisely or not, may always be discussed. But, at all events, her decision finally secured England's insular position and all that springs from it. It is interesting to consider what might have been; but, in so doing, we always construct our own results, though we cannot trace in other events the same logical sequence as we assume in our own calculations. It is enough for the delineation of Elizabeth's character to make clear the conclusion to which she arrived. She was not allured by any hope of glory; she did not aspire to military fame; she had no enthusiasm for a great cause. She was no Amazon, but a careful housewife. She provided for the present and left the future to care for itself. Further, the only interests which she considered were those of England, and the heroism of the Netherlands did not move her. She did not sympathise with rebellion against a lawful sovereign, but with the claim of a people to determine their own religion. The revolt of the Netherlands supplied another piece which she could play in her cautious game. She felt fully justified in playing it as suited her own purposes.

So while she declined the sovereignty of the States, she was reluctantly compelled to give them some assistance, that they might not fall before Spain at a time which was inconvenient to herself. But she meant that her help should be as little as possible, and that her intervention should prepare the way for ultimate peace. She wished, as usual, to be economical, and demanded that some of the seaport towns should be garrisoned by English soldiers till she had been repaid all that she had spent. Then she issued a "Declaration of the Causes moving the Queen of England to give aid to the defence of the people of the Low Countries". In this remarkable document she was careful to minimise the extent and object of her intervention. She rehearsed the ancient connection between England and the Netherlands, the causes of the revolt, and her continual advice to the King of Spain that he should respect the ancient liberties of the people. She then spoke of England's grievances against Spain, and the danger which would ensue if the Netherlands were reduced to a Spanish province. For these causes she had resolved "to send certain companies of soldiers to aid the national people of those countries, only to defend them and their towns from sacking and desolation, and thereby to procure them safety to enjoy their ancient liberties, and so to preserve the ancient commerce betwixt our people and those countries". The object which she had in view was "a deliverance of them from war by the Spaniards and foreigners, with a restitution of their ancient liberties and government by some Christian peace". In fact, she hoped by a demonstration of force to induce Spain to make terms with the Netherlands. She did not say, what she meant, that she and not the Netherlanders was to be judge of what terms were desirable.

The English commander was the Earl of Leicester, a man without military experience, chosen merely as a representative of the Queen, and not likely to err through over-activity. The expedition was merely to cover Elizabeth's diplomacy, and was to be as little warlike as might be. But such slackness did not approve itself to Elizabeth's ministers, and they saw an opportunity of forcing her hand. Leicester was vain and unstable; he chafed at his own helplessness, and made an effort to burst his bonds. When he arrived in the Netherlands, in January, 1586, he accepted in the Queen's name the office of Governor of the States and took an oath to observe their liberties. Great was Elizabeth's wrath when this news reached her. It was aggravated by the information that Lady Leicester proposed to join her husband with a suite of attendants. Elizabeth declared that she "would have no Courts under her obeisance save her own". Leicester was ordered to lay aside his office as best he could; and the beginning of English interference was only fruitful of uncertainty and perplexity. Leicester wrote sadly to the Queen: "I see my service is not acceptable, but rather more and more disliketh you. Here I can do your Majesty no service; there I can do you some, at the least, rub your horses' heels—a service which shall be much more welcome to me than this." When the Queen somewhat relented, he wrote: "My wounded heart is by this means almost made whole, and I do pray unto God that either I may never feel the like from you again, or not be suffered to live, rather than I should fall again into those torments of your displeasure". His only comfort was in "reposing evermore under the shadow of those blessed beams that must yield the only nourishment to this disease".

While Leicester was thus making peace with his mistress he had no energy to make war upon the enemy. His command in the Netherlands was inglorious, marked only by a skirmish round Zutphen, which is remembered because it cost the life of Sir Philip Sidney. His military operations were crippled by want of funds, and he was not fortunate in winning the affection of the people whom he undertook to govern. In November, 1586, his presence was required in England, and he departed unregretted.

But if Leicester's exploits did not contribute to the reduction of the power of Spain, there was another Englishman engaged in another form of warfare who was more successful, Francis Drake. Philip had attempted to stop English interference in the Netherlands by a sudden seizure of all English ships in Spanish harbours. While the anger which this caused was still hot, Drake obtained from the Queen permission to equip a squadron for another adventure in the Spanish Main. Already English seamen had begun to despise the Spaniards and look on Philip as "a colossus stuffed with clouts". Drake landed in Vigo Bay to give the Spaniards a lesson. Having taken all the spoil he could, he sailed for the Western Sea, where he took by assault the towns of St. Iago, San Domingo and Cartagena. This was a more serious matter than the capture of ships at sea. It warned the Spaniards that their colonies were not secure. "England," said one of them, "has many teeth." Elizabeth probably counted more on the exploits of Drake than on those of Leicester to induce Philip to make peace with the Netherlands, an object which she steadily pursued. She regarded her position in the Netherlands as a means of enforcing such terms as she thought satisfactory, even if they did not satisfy the States themselves.

If Elizabeth was hopeful by this tortuous policy of averting war, her ministers did not share her expectation. They felt that a crisis was approaching and were determined to prepare for it. They were under no illusion as regarded their own position: they knew that the death of the Queen meant their death also. It is one of the remarkable features of Elizabeth's policy that she never attempted to form a party of her own. She insisted on being Queen of all her people, and did not attempt to raise a body of adherents. Her favourites were avowedly and openly personal, and were not admitted to her most secret councils. She welcomed all at Court, and used their services as she thought fit. Her ministers might advise her, but she acted for herself. Burghley and Walsingham, who were her ablest and most trusty servants, were kept in a position of absolute dependence on her will. They were not enriched or exalted to high positions. There was no prominent man who could claim to take the lead, no one whom others would follow. The bond of association had attempted to make provision for a crisis; but its method was felt to be cumbrous, and its practical value was doubtful. It was inevitable that those who served Elizabeth should have some regard for their own safety. They were the instruments of all that had been done; they would be held responsible for it in the future; what was the future to be? Even behind the walls of Tutbury Mary Queen of Scots was not entirely safe. They thought of all the possible machinations

of foreign and domestic foes, and trembled. Every year that
Mary lived they were more deeply committed against her, and
most surely exposed to her revenge. Her existence was an intolerable menace which haunted them continually.

Walsingham had devoted himself with rare skill and success
to the work of discovering the plots which were being devised
against the Queen. He wished to prove Mary's complicity in
some form or other. At first the object in removing Mary to
Tutbury, and cutting off her communications with her friends,
had been to render her harmless. Walsingham proposed to prove
her harmful. For this purpose he devised an ingenious plan by
which Mary might think that she was outwitting her guardian,
whereas all her correspondence passed through Walsingham's
hands. This plan was carried out, and Elizabeth was enabled to
gratify her curiosity by reading Mary's letters. But, after a few
months, a letter addressed to Mary contained indications of a
conspiracy against the Queen's life: "There be means in hand to
remove the beast that troubles all the world". The head of this
conspiracy was a Jesuit, John Ballard; its chief organiser was
Antony Babington, a gentleman of Derbyshire, who had associated with him other young men of family and position.

Enough was soon known to justify the seizure of Ballard and
Babington; but Elizabeth chose to run the risk of assassination for
some weeks till the entire story was slowly unravelled. When
Walsingham's spy, who was "attending Mary's very heart," was
satisfied that he had learned all he could, the toils closed round
the conspirators. Mary's papers were seized during her absence
and were sent to London. Walsingham had obtained evidence
which must lead of necessity to a judicial investigation. All this
had gone on with such bewildering rapidity that even Elizabeth
herself was startled by the issue which had been suddenly raised.
She saw, when it was too late, that Walsingham had practically
forced her hand. The conspirators must be tried, and Mary's letters must be produced. This would necessitate a decision about
Mary—a decision which Elizabeth had long deferred, be-

cause it was fraught with danger. She could not escape from appointing a Commission of peers and judges to try Mary under the provisions of the recent Act for the protection of the Queen against such as should raise rebellion. On October 25, 1586, Mary was found guilty of "compassing divers matters tending to the hurt and destruction of the Queen".

Parliament met in November, and petitioned for the publication of the sentence. Elizabeth answered in a speech which was entirely free from her accustomed ambiguities, and expressed her deepest and noblest thoughts. She thanked God for His mercies, and thanked her people for their loyalty. She grieved at the treachery to which she had been exposed, and most of all that Mary had been a party to it. "Even yet, though the matter be come thus far, if she would truly repent, and no man would undertake her cause against me, and if my life alone depended hereupon, and not the welfare of my people, I would willingly pardon her. Nay, if England by my death might obtain a more flourishing condition, and a better Prince, I would most gladly lay down my life. For it is for my people's sake that I desire to live. As for me, I see no such great reason why I should either be fond to live or fear to die. I have had good experience of this world. I have known what it is to be a subject, and I now know what it is to be a sovereign. Good neighbours I have had, and I have met with bad; and in trust I have found treason. I have bestowed benefits on ill-deservers; and where I have done well, I have been ill-requited and spoken of. While I call to mind things past, behold things present, and look forward towards things to come, I count them happiest that go hence soonest. Nevertheless, against such evils and mischiefs as these, I am armed with a better courage than is common in my sex: so as whatsoever befals me, death shall never find me unprepared." She could not avoid proceeding against Mary under the late Act, but she had chosen the noblest and most learned in the land to form a Commission: "For we Princes are set as it were upon stages in the sight and view of all the world. The least spot is soon seen in our garments, the

smallest blemish presently observed in us at a great distance."
The decision of the Commission had reduced her to great perplexity, and she asked for time to consider what to do.

In fact, Elizabeth's position was very difficult. It was not her
own interest to put Mary to death. So long as Mary was safe in
her hands, she was free, at least, from other claimants to the
throne, and those who wished for the old state of things in England could wait for the chance of Mary's accession. Yet the removal of Mary would be a great relief to England; for if Elizabeth died first, Mary's claim to succeed could not be resisted. So
Elizabeth was called upon to do what she did not wish to do; and,
moreover, the responsibility of doing it must rest entirely with
herself. Elizabeth had spent her life in studiously avoiding the
obligation of making up her mind, in putting off a decision till a
decision had become unnecessary, because things had settled
themselves. Now she was face to face with a question which must
be decided one way or the other. At first she tried to escape, and
sent to Parliament asking them to find out another way. The answer was returned that "as it was injustice to deny execution of
the law to any of her subjects that should demand it so much
more to the whole body of her people of England, unanimously
and with one voice humbly and instantly suing for the same".
Again Elizabeth answered: "Very unpleasing is that way, where
the setting out, progress and journey's end yield nothing but
trouble and vexation. I cannot but complain, though not of you,
yet to you, that my safety depends on the ruin of another."
Parliament was prorogued without a decided answer.

The conduct of Elizabeth about the execution of Mary shows
her at her worst. It was a vain attempt to apply her habitual
course of action to a case which did not allow it. She did not wish
to put Mary to death; but still more she did not wish to have the
responsibility either of doing it or of refusing to do it. To refuse
was to cast a doubt upon the justice of all the executions which
had hitherto been deemed necessary. Jesuits and priests had been
put to death for being privy to plots against the Queen: on what

ground could Mary be spared? To assert now that Mary was a monarch over whom the English Queen had no jurisdiction, was to give her a recognition which had hitherto been studiously denied. At first Elizabeth tried to wring from Mary some expression of repentance and promise for the future; but Mary loudly maintained her innocence and would admit nothing. After wavering for some time, Elizabeth at last signed the warrant for her execution, but suggested to the Secretary, Davison, that it would be a great relief to her if some loyal subject were to kill Mary in pursuance of the oath of the association, now sanctioned by Act of Parliament; Sir Amyas Paulet and Sir Drew Drury, who had charge of Mary at Fotheringay, might perhaps act on this suggestion. Paulet replied, as might have been expected, that "his goods and life were at Her Majesty's disposal, but he would not make shipwreck of his conscience, or leave so great a blot to his posterity as shed blood without law or warrant". Elizabeth was angry at this answer, denounced the "niceness of those precise fellows," and complained of their perjury, because contrary to their oath they threw the burden upon her, "swearing a great oath, that it was a shame for us all that it was not already done, considering that she had, for her part, done all that law or reason could require of her". Again Elizabeth was desperately struggling to avoid a decision, by making suggestions which were not only dishonourable but palpably absurd. She might send aid to the Netherlands, and then deny it; but she could not put Mary to death and yet deny that she had done so. She might send Drake to the Spanish Main, on the understanding that she might disavow him if he failed; but she could not expect her most loyal subjects to undertake Mary's slaughter, with the knowledge that she would disavow them if they succeeded.

Every one around her understood her position; and Burghley hoped to divide the responsibility. He called a meeting of the Council, which was unanimous that the sentence should be carried out. The warrant was sent to Fotheringay, and Mary's head fell on the block on February 18, 1587. No sooner did the news reach Elizabeth than she counterfeited extreme sorrow, and vehement indignation. She accused Davison of betraying her, and committed him to the Tower. She wrote to Scotland and to France that she was innocent of Mary's death. No one believed her, but she continued to protest. Burghley was not allowed to approach her for two months, and then was overwhelmed with abuse. Davison was tried by a commission, which, while acquitting him of evil intent, convicted him of abuse of trust, and imposed a fine of ten thousand marks, with imprisonment at the Queen's pleasure. No one supposed that this sentence would be carried out; but Elizabeth had embarked on a course which she felt bound to pursue. Davison was imprisoned for three years, the fine was exacted, and when he was released from the Tower he was a ruined man. This miserable injustice was all to no purpose. No one believed Elizabeth one whit the more.

Her action at this crisis was only an exhibition on a conspicuous scale of her habitual conduct. She wished to seem to regulate affairs without really doing so. When something had to be done, she wished it to be done so as not to commit her to continue on that course unless it was convenient. The execution of Mary was a necessity towards which she had drifted against her will. She thought that she could not escape it without risking her popularity and endangering her personal safety. She shrunk from it, not only because it was a stain on her name, and a breach of her own conception of what was due to a royal personage, but because it must necessarily change the political position of England, and make it much more decided than it was before. Hitherto Elizabeth had tried to hold a balance, and to keep the future uncertain by refusing to regulate the succession to the Crown. This was destroyed by Mary's death, which removed the chance of a Roman Catholic successor, who would have been inclined to France rather than Spain. While Mary lived, Philip had only a languid interest in combating heresy in England. Now that she was gone, he could claim the English throne for himself.

Elizabeth tried to minimise the political results of Mary's

death, and pursued more keenly than before her plan of making peace for the Netherlands. Again she tried her old method, an armed demonstration in the Low Countries, secret negotiations with the Prince of Parma, and pressure on Spain by maritime enterprise. In April, 1587, Drake sailed into Cadiz Bay, destroyed a great number of transports and store-ships, and then did the same in the harbour of Lisbon. Philip was secretly gathering stores for an expedition against England; Drake suspected his design and crippled him for the present. Philip, however, soon repaired the damage, and, had the Armada set out in the autumn, England would have been unprepared for resistance. But Philip delayed, and mishaps were many. It was not till the summer of 1588 that the Armada was ready to set sail.

It is not necessary to tell again the story of the defeat of the Armada. Its event justified the opinion, which English sailors had already formed, that "twelve of Her Majesty's ships were a match for all the galleys in the King of Spain's dominions". The real danger lay in the possibility of the Spanish fleet uniting with Parma, and so providing means of transporting the veteran troops of Spain to England. But the English spirit was now fully awake. If the death of Mary had quickened Philip's zeal for the conquest of England, it had united all classes of Englishmen against annexation to Spain. When the time of peril came, England was practically one in its loyalty to the Queen, and its great anxiety was the protection of her person. It is curious to observe how seldom the real meaning of a crisis is understood. England was not so much afraid of the Spanish fleet as of the possible landing of the Prince of Parma. It did not fear for its command of the sea, but for its internal peace. It was more concerned in military preparations on shore than in the equipment of the fleet. The men of England were called out under arms, 100,000 strong. The levies of the Midlands, to the number of 30,000, were appointed as a guard of the Queen's person. The rest were to gather where danger menaced. It seemed natural that the Earl of Leicester should be put in command of the forces.

The troops who were to defend London and the Queen took up their position at Tilbury to guard the spot where the Thames could most easily be crossed. They assembled full of ardour. "It was a pleasant sight," says a contemporary writer, "to behold the soldiers as they marched towards Tilbury, their cheerful countenances, courageous words and gestures, dancing and leaping wheresoever they came; and, in the camp, their most felicity was hope of fight with the enemy, where ofttimes divers rumours ran of their foe's approach, and that present battle would be given them. Then were they as joyful at such news as if lusty giants were to run a race." Elizabeth visited the camp at Tilbury and kindled a passion of loyalty in the breasts of her defenders. Certainly few sovereigns have known how to act their part in public with such unerring tact as did Elizabeth. Mounted upon a war-horse, Bellona-like, with a general's truncheon in her hand, wearing a breastplate of burnished steel, and attended by a page who bore her helmet, she rode bare-headed through the ranks. Then, with clear resonant voice, she addressed her soldiers in such terms as went straight to the heart of each. "My loving people, we have been persuaded by some that are careful of our safety, to take heed how we commit ourselves to armed multitudes for fear of treachery. But assure you, I do not desire to live to distrust my faithful and loving people. Let tyrants fear. I have always so behaved myself that, under God, I have placed my chiefest strength and safeguard in the loyal hearts and good will of my subjects. And therefore I am come among you at this time, not as for any recreation or sport, but being resolved, in the midst of the heat and the battle, to live or die amongst you all; to lay down for my God, and for my kingdom, and for my people, my honour and my blood, even in the dust. I know I have but the body of a weak and feeble woman; but I have the heart of a King, and of a King of England, too; and think foul scorn that Parma or Spain, or any prince of Europe, should dare to invade the borders of my realm. To which rather than any dishonour should grow by me, I my-

self will take up arms; I myself will be your general, judge and
rewarder of every one of your virtues in the field."

There was no affectation in such words as these. Elizabeth
could always, in an emergency, appeal to her people to recognise
the fundamental principles of her government. She was the protector of her country, the prudent executor of its will. Where
she erred, it was because she did not clearly see what her people
really desired. She had to supply their lack of foresight, and had
to interpret their inarticulate wishes. She had no personal interests which were contrary to theirs. She could appeal to them to
recognise that she and they were indissolubly united, and they
ever responded to the appeal.

Though the muster at Tilbury was a sign of the spirit of Englishmen, the work was done by the mariners whom Hawkins
and Drake had trained. They gave the strongest expression to the
national temper, which had slowly grown under Elizabeth's
fostering care, and which the threat of invasion roused to a sudden
consciousness of its strength. The land forces were not called
upon to fight for their country; but we can well believe that
"they prayed heartily the Spaniards might land quickly; and
when they knew they were fled, they began to lament". The defeat of the Armada showed England that its true defence must
depend upon its power at sea. Much has been said about Elizabeth's parsimony, and want of adequate preparations for the
navy. That Elizabeth exacted strict economy in all public matters
is most certain; but she was not personally responsible for the
equipment or victualling of the fleet, and did not interfere with
her officials. Money was freely given, and such arrangements
were made as were possible. But there was no system of com-
missariat in existence; it was hard to provide for adequate supplies
of food, nor could the ships carry any great stores. It would seem
that everything was done that could be done; but sickness broke
out on board the ships, and many of the sailors died. The Queen
committed to Burghley and Walsingham the duty of providing

for the public service. They knew that she would exact a strict account, and they kept a careful watch over all subordinates. Strict regularity in accounts is always unpleasant, till the method of keeping them is discovered and the habit is established. The Admiral Lord Howard, and the Controller Sir John Hawkins, both found some difficulty in producing their accounts for audit. The demand that they should do so marks the beginning of greater efficiency in administration, and a higher standard of honour in dealing with public money. Elizabeth scarcely deserves in this matter the reproach of unworthy parsimony.

VII

THE NEW ENGLAND

◆§ Proving the success of the method which Elizabeth had studiously followed, the defeat of the Armada marked the decisive epoch of her reign. She had found the country dispirited, divided and uncertain. She had refused to answer definitely any of the problems by which it was distracted. She was contented to maintain government, to defend her own position against attack and to occupy the position of moderator between contending parties. The one thing which she strove to avoid was an outburst of strong feeling, or aught that would divide England into opposite camps. Her great belief was that England would grow into a new consciousness of its position, if it had time for reflection and for experiment. However much questions might seem pressing for solution, she refused to solve them. However loudly the popular voice might clamour for action, she devised means of seeming to act without really doing so. England must decide for itself, and she would be the ruler over a united people. It was only when opinions led to disloyalty that she repressed them. Her only demand was that England should not be sacrificed to the issues raised by Continental politics, but should find its own course of safety. From this determination nothing could move her, and she had her reward. She secured peace as long as peace was possible; but the growth of the English spirit at last challenged attack. When the attack came, England was practically united. Roman Catholics were not behind their brethren in loyalty. The time was past when they were willing to secure their own form of religion at the price of the sacrifice of England to Spain. This was because England had a meaning for them which it had not for their fathers. Elizabeth, who at the beginning of her reign was regarded as a temporary makeshift, a creature who could be removed at any moment when it was convenient, had become the representative of a great nation, which rejoiced in its independence, and had gained a conception of order and liberty which formed the foundation of a strong national life. The attack, which had so long been dreaded, was delivered and was easily repulsed.

The effect of this repulse on England was enormous. Confidence had been gradually growing; now it came at once to light. Englishmen knew that they could hold their own, and had a foremost place in the world. The haunting sense of uncertainty passed away, and they were able to face the future. It was this knowledge, coming in all its freshness, which set its stamp upon the Elizabethan age. It was when Elizabeth's work was done that her worth was recognised, and she became the symbol of the nation which she had done so much to create. Men forgave her everything in the past because they saw something of the meaning of her views, and acknowledged their obligation to much that had disappointed them at the time when it was done, or more often left undone. They even attributed to her counsels the defeat of the Armada itself, and struck a medal with the inscription *"Dux faemina facti"*.

The new generation which had grown up around Elizabeth was very different from that which was passing away. The men of the older generation were cautious, prudent and self-restrained. They had been trained amid perpetual dangers, and had learned to walk warily, to say as little as possible, and to trust entirely to no one. Their followers were outspoken, adventurous and turbulent, overflowing with life and energy. The question must have faced Elizabeth, Could she restrain them, as she had restrained their fathers? How was she to carry into the new England the authority and influence which she had exercised over the old? Her power had been largely due to her personal ascendancy, and she needed a life full of personal interests. She preserved her intellectual coldness by gratifying her feelings. She dominated her ministers by pampering her favourites. She learned to understand the world around her, not only through her head, but through her heart. She was a woman as well as a Queen, and did not sink herself in her office. She reserved self-restraint for important decisions; in matters of everyday life she followed her own fancy. It is strange that increasing age and experience did not teach her to curb her personal preferences. But she was one of those who were resolved to lead their individual lives in their own way, and to exercise their qualities on those immediately around them.

It was almost a sign of the new epoch opening in England that the Earl of Leicester died on September 4, 1588. Though he had never seriously affected Elizabeth's policy, he had always retained a hold on her affections. She had felt his charm, and had been delighted by his accomplishments. When he grew presumptuous, he was repressed; but the Queen chose that he should be reckoned as the foremost man in England. It was a position which he in no way deserved; but it was not Elizabeth's habit to reward desert. Some one must occupy the chief place in her Court. There was a time when she would have married Leicester; as that could not be, at least he should have some recompense. So he continued to be an important figure, though he was not entrusted with any real power.

It would seem, however, that before his death he had thought of a possible successor. Elizabeth's fancy was more and more interested in the young, and she loved to hear their ideas and aspirations. She chose those to whom she wished to listen for their personal appearance, just as the whim took her. Thus, when she saw young Charles Blount, "Of stature tall and of very comely proportion," she said to him, significantly: "Fail you not to come to Court, and I will bethink myself how to do you good". In like manner, Walter Raleigh had attracted her attention by his "good presence, in a handsome and well-compacted person, a strong natural wit, and a bold and plausible tongue". Leicester knew that he himself, owing to advancing years and self-indulgence, was growing "high-coloured and red-faced". Not wishing to be entirely at the mercy of his younger rivals, he introduced another aspirant for the Queen's favour, his step-son, Robert Devereux, Earl of Essex. Already in May, 1587, we find that the brilliant youth of twenty had ousted his competitors. "When the Queen is abroad, nobody is near her but my Lord of Essex; and at night, my Lord is at cards, or one game or another with her that he cometh not to his own lodging till the birds sing in the morning." In July Essex was on such terms that he upbraided the Queen for refusing to receive his sister, who had made a runaway marriage, and said "that it was only to please that knave Raleigh, for whose sake I saw she would both grieve me and my love, and disgrace me in the eye of the world". When he did not receive the satisfaction which he demanded, he rode away to join the Earl of Leicester in the Netherlands; but Elizabeth sent a messenger in pursuit, and he was brought back from the coast before he could embark.

After Leicester's death Essex was regarded as his undoubted successor in the Queen's good graces. Raleigh retired to Ireland, and Essex tried to rid himself of Blount. Seeing him wearing a favour which Elizabeth had given him in the tilt, Essex contemptuously said: "Now I perceive that every fool must wear a favour". A duel followed, and Essex was wounded. Elizabeth asked the reason of his absence, and when she heard the cause, exclaimed: "By God's death, it were fitting some one should take him down, and teach him better manners, or there were no rule with him". She was not displeased that two young men should quarrel for her good graces; but she reproved them both, and insisted on a reconciliation, which in this case proved lasting.

The ideas and objects of such a man as Essex were entirely those of the new generation, and had little in common with the policy which Elizabeth had hitherto pursued. Her old counsellors were dropping off. Walsingham died in 1590, and Burghley alone remained to represent the traditions of the past. It was a question what policy should now be pursued. England was at war with

Spain; how should that war be waged? It was in England's power to decide. Spain could not assail her; should she assail Spain? It was possible to weaken Spain by raids upon its coasts, and attacks upon its shipping, till Spain was ready to make peace on satisfactory terms. It was also possible to attack the Spanish Empire beyond the seas, and set up an English Empire in its stead. This was the wish of the adventurous spirits who represented the new England, men trained in the school of Drake, and desirous of framing a line of action in imitation of his exploits. Those who knew Elizabeth knew that she would not be enticed into any great undertaking, but would pursue peace on advantageous terms. Yet she would not set herself against any strong current of feeling. She found room for it, and gave it expectations; she studied it carefully, that she might know how to restrain it within cautious limits. She allowed it to make a few experiments, when they were not costly.

So in April, 1589, she allowed an expedition to set out against Spain for the restoration of Don Antonio to the throne of Portugal. Drake, Norris, and a few private adventurers undertook the main expense; Elizabeth only lent some ships, and contributed towards the adventure, the profits of which were to be shared amongst the subscribers. They first attacked Coruña, and then set sail for Lisbon. On the way they were joined by Essex, who this time managed to escape the Queen's vigilance. But the Portuguese did not rise in favour of Don Antonio; sickness set in among the troops and the expedition was a failure, though it inflicted considerable loss on Spain.

Essex returned home, and was forgiven for his escapade, though he had transgressed the law in leaving England without the Queen's permission. It was for such an offence that the luckless Earl of Arundel had been committed to the Tower. But Arundel had apparently incurred the Queen's condign displeasure, and was tried for treason because he had added to his offences by praying in the Tower for the success of the Armada. It would seem that he and a priest had met for continuous prayer during the period of danger, though Arundel asserted that their prayer was for protection against massacre, which was threatened against all Romanists if the Spaniards made good their landing. He was found guilty and was condemned to death. The sentence was not carried into effect, but the axe was kept hanging over his head till his death six years later. He was not allowed to see his wife and child, and was treated with exceptional severity. It would seem that Elizabeth could not brook Arundel's attitude of quiet resignation. She had no sympathy with what she considered to be mere obstinacy, and treated it with the utmost rigour.

If England had been given to magnificent entertainments in the Queen's honour previously, there was an increase of pageantry in the years that followed on the national triumph. In 1589 Sir Henry Lee, who had held the post of the Queen's champion, resigned in favour of the Earl of Cumberland. When the jousts were over, Sir Henry led Cumberland to the Queen, while a hidden minstrel sang of the physical evils of advancing age, though the devotion of the heart remained still fresh. As the song went on, there came from the ground a temple of the Vestal Virgins, imitating white marble and porphyry. Within it stood an altar laden with gifts, and on a pillar a votive tablet "To Eliza". The gifts were reverently offered to the Queen. Lee was disarmed, and his armour laid before Elizabeth; then he knelt and prayed her to take Cumberland in his stead. On receiving her assent he armed Cumberland and set him on his horse, while he himself donned the cloak of a civilian.

George Clifford, Earl of Cumberland, was famed for his knightly bearing and his personal courage. He was handsome, magnificent and extravagant, like the rest of the young courtiers, amongst whom the love of adventure was enforced by the desire to make, or mend, their fortunes. It was a hard task for Elizabeth to keep them within limits, and her fantastic method of attaching them personally to herself was only the application to a new state of things of the method which she had previously pursued. So long as Mary lived, Elizabeth tried to identify the chief men of England with her service in a personal way, that so they might feel themselves committed to her fortunes. Now that she was undoubted Queen, and a representative of the nation to a degree that none of her predecessors had been, she used the prevailing enthusiasm to make herself not only officially, but personally, supreme. She drew into her own hands the disposal of every man's fortunes, and demanded an unbounded devotion to herself, as preliminary to any occupation in State affairs. Hence she resented the marriage of any of her favourites without her leave, and tried to exalt her own politic celibacy into a universal model. Her effort was unavailing. In 1590 the Earl of Essex secretly married Frances Walsingham, widow of Philip Sidney, to Elizabeth's great vexation. Later, Raleigh married Elizabeth, daughter of Sir Nicholas Throgmorton, and was committed to the Tower by the indignant Queen. The sight of Elizabeth in her barge so moved him that he begged his keeper to allow him to disguise himself and "get into a pair of oars to ease his mind but with the sight of the Queen, or else his heart would break". When his request was refused, he drew his dagger and behaved like a madman—knowing that the story would be related to the Queen. He wrote to Robert Cecil: "I that was wont to behold her riding like Alexander, hunting like Diana, walking like Venus, the gentle air blowing her fair hair about her pure cheeks, like a nymph; sometimes sitting in the shade like a goddess; sometimes singing like an angel; sometimes playing like Orpheus. Behold the sorrow of the world! Once amiss hath bereaved me of all." There was as much policy as folly in exacting such language as this from such fiery and undisciplined spirits as Raleigh and Essex.

There were, however, affairs of moment to be settled on the Continent. The murder of Henry III. of France had left the Bourbon, Henry of Navarre, heir to the French throne; but the league refused to admit the title of a Huguenot King, and was supported by Spain. Elizabeth took up the same position towards Henry as she had so long held towards the rebellion in the

Netherlands; she would send him money for warfare by land, and would annoy Spain by naval expeditions, but would give him no definite assistance. Essex vainly tried to induce her to send some troops to France; but Elizabeth refused, until the news that the Prince of Parma was going to the help of the league compelled her to avert a catastrophe. Essex knelt before her for hours, imploring the command of the English forces; but Elizabeth chose an old and experienced captain, Sir John Norris, to serve in Brittany. Afterwards Essex was sent with an additional force of 4000 men to press the siege of Rouen, before Henry went to meet Parma. Little was done by the English forces. Essex was summoned home to allay Elizabeth's anxiety when she heard of his foolhardy doings. He was allowed to return, but the Council wrote to him charging him "that you do not attempt, by no persuasions, nor for respect of any vainglory, to put in danger your own person at this siege of Rouen". Such an order to the general did not show any desire for vigorous operations; and so little energy was displayed by the French that Essex was recalled early in 1592, and the seige of Rouen was abandoned.

The death of Walsingham, in 1590, had marked another great breach with the past. Few men have ever shown more capacity and skill in obtaining political information. He organised a secret service in all the Courts of Europe, and cautiously kept in his hand the clue to everything that was happening. We have seen that he was the only one amongst her ministers who ever succeeded in forcing Elizabeth to act with decision. Elizabeth, much as she owed to his services, resented his success over herself. She gave him little reward, and he died a poor man. His death raised the question of his succession, which became a bone of contention between Essex and Burghley. Burghley wished to advance to the post his son, Robert Cecil; Essex was unfortunate in his candidate for he chose Davison, the secretary who had been dismissed. Yet Essex's choice was both chivalrous and worthy, as Davison was a man of proved sagacity. Elizabeth rejected Davison, but so far humoured Essex as not to fill the vacant post.

During the absence of Essex, "the old fox," as Essex called Burghley, pursued his plan for the advancement of his son. He entertained the Queen at his house at Theobalds, where Robert Cecil was knighted. A few months afterwards he was sworn of the Privy Council, and was appointed secretary. He celebrated the occasion by a performance before the Queen, which was eminently characteristic of the man. He was small in stature, with a slight curvature of the spine, and had no hopes of vieing with the Queen's favourites. He could only commend himself to her by his official capacity, as the inheritor to his father's traditions and the representative of that policy which had been so successful in the past. So he took the occasion of complimenting the Queen, not on her beauty, but on her wisdom; and he protested his devotion, not so much to her person, as to her policy. A dialogue took place in the Queen's presence between a postman and an usher of the Secretary's. The post came in haste bearing a letter from the Emperor of China. The secretary was not to be found; what was to be done? The usher advised the delivery of the letter to the Queen herself. "What then," asked the post, "is the use of servants?" "She makes use of them," was the answer, "as the mind does of the senses. Many things she sees and hears through them; but the judgment and election is her own." "Why, if this be all, is their reward so great?" "Oh, therein she respects her own greatness and goodness, which must need be what it is, though it find no object that is proportionable. Like a gentle mistress of children, she guides their hand and thereby makes them write fair letters, the yet to encourage them, praises them as if they had done it without direction." On hearing this the post was about to deliver his letter to the Queen, but was stopped by the consideration that it is written in a strange language which she will not understand. The usher assured him that "she speaks and understands all the languages in the world which are worthy to be spoken or understood". "It may be," said the post, "that she understands them in a sort well for a lady, but not as secretaries should do." "What talk you of secretaries?" exclaimed the usher. "As for one of them whom you most ask for, if he have anything that is worth talking of, the world knows well enough where he had it; for he kneels every day where he learns a new lesson." The post is daunted by the thought of appearing before so much wisdom and majesty, and thinks that it will be safer for him to seek out the secretary. The usher stops him, "Ah, simple post, thou art the wilfullest creature that liveth. Dost thou not know that, besides all her perfections, all the earth hath not such a prince of affability? For all is one; come gentleman, come serving man, come ploughman, come beggar, the hour is yet to come that ever she refuseth petition." Overcome by this assurance, the post plucked up courage and delivered his letter to the Queen. Cecil might indeed rest contented with the knowledge that there were sides of Elizabeth's character, to which he could appeal, which lay beyond the reach of his more brilliant rivals. They were bent upon their own designs, and were struggling to draw the Queen further than she intended to go. She, on her part, was endeavouring to curb their soaring ambition, and for this purpose she needed the official devotion of Cecil, that so she might keep the balance nicely hung, and still retain her hold upon the new aspirations of England.

For this purpose she increased her state, and multiplied her progresses. They were useful as bringing her into connection with different parts of her domains. They were useful also as inciting her nobility to extravagant expenditure, and so making them more dependent on her goodwill. In the summer of 1591 she visited Lord Montague at Cowdray in Sussex. On her arrival, Lady Montague wept on her bosom, exclaiming: "Oh happy time! oh joyful day!" There was a bower erected in the park, near paddocks filled with deer. A nymph offered a crossbow to the Queen, who shot three or four. A pilgrim met her in the wood and led her to a tree, whereon her arms and those of all her suite were splendidly emblazoned on escutcheons. Soon afterwards she visited the Earl of Hertford at Elvetham. Hertford had the reputation of being the wealthiest man in England, and his preparations were correspondingly magnificent. A poet met her with a Latin oration. The three Graces and the three Hours cleared the way of stumbling blocks which had been laid by Envy, and then escorted her to the house with songs of welcome. An artificial pond had been constructed in the shape of a half moon. Seated under a canopy of green satin, the Queen beheld Nereus, Oceanus, and Tritons disporting themselves on its waters, and indulging in appropriate songs. Sylvanus advanced from the woods, making uncouth love to a water nymph; he was pulled into the water and mocked by the river gods. Nereus and Neaera both presented the Queen with costly jewels from their watery realm. On islands in the pond there were displays of fireworks. The Queen of fairyland assembled her maidens to dance in the garden, and greeted Elizabeth in song:—

> *Elisa is the fairest Queen*
> *That ever trod upon this green;*
> *Elisa's eyes are blessed stars,*
> *Inducing peace, subduing wars;*
> *Elisa's hand is christal bright;*
> *Her words are balm; her looks are light;*
> *Elisa's breast is that fair hill*
> *Where virtue dwells and sacred skill.*
> *O blessed be each day and hour*
> *Where sweet Elisa builds her bower.*

On her departure a band of musicians hidden in a bower sang in sad strains:—

> *O come again, fair nature's treasure*
> *Whose looks yield joys exceeding measure.*
> *O come again, Heaven's chief delight,*
> *Thine absence makes eternal night;*

O come again world's star-bright eye,
Whose presence doth adorn the sky;
O come again, sweet beauty's sun;
When thou art gone, our joys are done.

We cannot wonder that Elizabeth "protested to my Lord of Hertford that the beginning, process and end of his entertainment was so honourable, as hereafter he should find the reward thereof in her special favour". Doubtless Elizabeth meant what she said; but Hertford had already expiated his offence of marrying Lady Catharine Grey by nine years' imprisonment in the Tower. Lady Catharine was now dead and Hertford had married the daughter of the Lord Admiral Howard. Elizabeth's anger was again kindled by discovering that, in 1585, Hertford had taken legal opinion about the validity of his first marriage and had caused it to be recorded in the Court of Arches. For this offence, committed years previously, he was again imprisoned, and doubtless had to purchase his release by a heavy fine.

In 1592 Elizabeth again paid several visits. At Sudeley she was entertained by Lord Chandos, who showed her Apollo pursuing Daphne, who entered into a tree, whence she emerged and took refuge with "the Queen of Charity". She also went to Oxford to do honour to the new Chancellor, Lord Buckhurst, who succeeded Hatton, to the great mortification of the Earl of Essex, who wished for that distinguished position. But Elizabeth was cautious in her bestowal of offices, and would not allow her favourite to accumulate power in his hands. At Oxford there was the usual provision of speeches, plays and disputations. One of the disputations was on the curious subject: "Whether it be lawful to dissemble in matters of religion?" The Bishop of Hereford spoke at such length that the Queen twice sent to ask him to cut short his oration. As it was carefully prepared, he was unable to curtail it. Next day the Queen addressed the University. As she was speaking, her eye fell on Burghley, standing with difficulty on his gouty legs. She stopped and ordered a stool to be brought for him. An adroit courtier told her "that she did it of purpose, to show that she could interrupt her speech and not be put out, although the Bishop of Hereford durst not adventure to do so, for a less matter, the day before".

From Oxford the Queen proceeded to Rycote, near Thame, where she visited Lord Norris. He was the son of the ill-fated man who was executed as the alleged lover of Anne Boleyn. The father of Lady Norris had shared with Bedingfield the duty of guarding Elizabeth in her youth when she was at Woodstock, and had treated her kindly. On both these grounds Elizabeth showed exceptional kindness to Norris and his wife. She used to call Lady Norris "her black crow," from the darkness of her complexion. Norris was the father of six sons, "a brood of spirited, martial men". Four of them were at that time serving the Queen in Ireland, France and the Netherlands. So Norris could afford to receive the Queen with expressions of plain outspoken familiar loyalty, which are refreshing among the quaint devices with which she was generally greeted. Her welcome was given by an old soldier, who said: "Vouchsafe, dread Sovereign, after so many smooth speeches of the Muses, to hear a rough-hewn tale of a soldier. We use not with words to amplify our conceits, and to plead forth by figures, but by deeds to show the loyalty of our hearts, and to make it good with our lives. My horse, mine armour, my shield, my sword, the riches of a young soldier, and an old soldier's relics, I should here offer to your Highness; but my four sons have stolen them from me vowing themselves to arms, and leaving me to my prayers. This is their resolution and my desire, that their lives may be employed wholly in your service, and their deaths be their vow's sacrifice—their deaths, the rumour whereof hath so often affrighted the Crow my wife, that her heart hath been as black as her feathers. I know not whether it be affection or fondness, but the Crow thinketh her own birds the fairest, because to her they are the dearest. And although nothing be more unfit to lodge your Majesty than a crow's nest, yet shall it be most happy to us that it is by your Highness made a phœnix' nest." The next day four letters, each containing an appropriate present, were delivered from the absent sons. An Irish servant brought one containing a dart of gold set with diamonds, with the motto: "I fly only for my Sovereign". A skipper coming from the Netherlands presented another with a key of gold set with diamonds, bearing the inscription: "I open only to you". A French page handed three letters—one meant to be a comic mistake, being a soldier's letter to his mistress—the others containing a golden sword set with diamonds and rubies, inscribed: "Drawn only in your defence," and a truncheon with a motto: "I do not command but under you".

In 1593 Elizabeth was reluctantly compelled to summon Parliament for the purpose of obtaining money to pay her troops in France. She felt that the control of Parliament had become more difficult now that England's position was secure; but she was resolved to maintain her old authority to the full. Hitherto she had asked for little money; now her demands considerably increased. England must be trained to pay the price of its enhanced greatness, and must at the same time be kept within the limits of due obedience to its Sovereign. There were two matters which the Queen had hitherto succeeded in keeping from Parliamentary control—the settlement of the succession, and the regulation of the Church.

Nothing is more curious in Elizabeth's career than the steadfastness with which she refused to allow of Parliamentary interference in ecclesiastical matters. She was determined that the large system which had approved itself at the beginning of her reign should be allowed to shape itself into accordance with the needs of the nation, and that time should be given it for that purpose. We have seen how great were the difficulties which beset the restoration of religious unity in England, how a Romanist party grew up which unfortunately had a political significance which the State deemed it impossible to overlook, how consequently attendance at the services of the Church became a test of loyalty. But, besides the Romanists, there was also a party which wished to go farther in the direction of Continental Protestantism. The Romanists stood aloof from the Church, and claimed only to go their own way. The Puritans aimed at transforming the Church into agreement with the system of Calvin, and they continued to raise one question after another. When the contest about vestments had succeeded in reducing ecclesiastical ornaments to the lowest point, the Puritans put forward the system of Church government which Calvin had set up. They were greatly aided by the action of the Papacy towards Elizabeth, which made the majority of Englishmen desirous to emphasise the breach with Rome. Thomas Cartwright, at Cambridge, advocated the abolition of Episcopacy, and the introduction of the Presbyterian system. This was entirely opposed to the principles which had hitherto prevailed in England; it passed beyond the bounds of legitimate discussion; it did not propose the adaptation, but the subversion, of the Church. So Elizabeth, by proclamation, ordered the Bishops to put in force the provisions of the Act of Uniformity, and secure that such opinions should not be taught by the clergy of the Church. She hoped that this question would soon pass away, and, on Parker's death, in 1575, appointed as Archbishop of Canterbury, Edward Grindal, who was known to be sympathetic with Puritan opinions. It soon appeared that these opinions found new means of expression in "exercises," or "prophesyings"—meetings, originally of clergy, to which the laity were soon admitted. Thus there was growing up another form of worship of the Genevan type by the side of the Church services. Elizabeth ordered that this should be put down. Grindal was slack in obeying the Queen's command, and was suspended from the exercise of his functions. Meanwhile, in various ways, efforts were steadily made by a section of the clergy to introduce stealthily something resembling the Presbyterian system of discipline.

After Grindal's death, in 1583, his successor, Whitgift, undertook the task of introducing order, and purging the system of the Church. The Puritans did not ask for toleration, they did not plead for freedom; but they claimed that the Church should be changed into something else, that its formularies should be disregarded, and that a rigid discipline should be introduced. For this purpose they took orders and held office in the Church, that they might use their position to subvert it. Whitgift was resolved to put a stop to this, and ordered that all the clergy should subscribe to three articles, affirming the Royal supremacy, the lawfulness of the Book of Common Prayer, and assent to the Thirty-nine Articles. In pursuance of this policy Whitgift issued articles of inquiry to the clergy, which they were requested to answer by virtue of their office. An outcry was immediately raised that the Inquisition was being introduced into England. Burghley wrote to Whitgift that "this judicial and canonical sifting of poor ministers is not to edify or reform. In charity I think they ought not to answer all these nice points, except they were very notorious offenders in Papistry or heresy." Whitgift, in reply, defended his action, and added: "I know your Lordship desireth the peace of the Church, but it cannot be procured after so long liberty and lack of discipline if a few persons, so meanly qualified as most of them, are countenanced against the whole state of the clergy". The House of Commons, in 1585, took the side of the Puritans, and made proposals for restricting the authority of the Bishops. These were set aside, and Elizabeth, in proroguing Parliament, peremptorily asserted that she would tolerate neither "presumption nor new fangledness". It was the duty of the Bishops to provide for the governance of the Church; and it was her duty to see that they amended such things as needed amendment.

That Elizabeth should have adopted this attitude at such a time shows that she was acting from deliberate conviction. It was in the great crisis of her reign, when all Europe was against her, when her life was in daily peril, when she had nothing to trust save the goodwill of her people. This she herself admitted. "No Prince can be surer tied or faster bound than I am with the link of your goodwill; yet one matter toucheth me so near, as I may not overskip, religion, the ground on which all other matters ought to take root, and being corrupted may mar all the tree." Why did she not increase her popularity by listening to the petition of the Commons? There was every motive to induce her to do so. All her advisers were in favour of doing so; but Elizabeth stood firm and accepted all the responsibility. It is often said that she was destitute of real religious feeling, and acted only from motives of policy. This view is not borne out by facts. Elizabeth possessed the qualities of the head more than those of the heart. She could not sympathise with earnestness which passed into fanaticism. In early life she had made up her own mind about the essential elements of personal religion, and did not over-estimate the significance of outward forms. But she had a keen sense of the meaning of religious systems in their relation to national life, and she saw the importance to England of becoming the seat of the Church of the New Learning, a Church which did not break with the past, but received all that had been continued by human intelligence towards understanding the errors of the old system, and the means to remove them. The system of the Church was to remain, and was to be as independent as possible. Henry VIII. was willing to assume functions which had been usurped by the Pope; Elizabeth was careful to go back to the position of the earlier Kings. She recognised in her Bishops greater powers than they were prepared to use. When Parker asked her aid she bade him act on his own authority. When she thought that authority was not exercised with sufficient firmness, she called attention to remissness. She had a higher conception of the Church than had the Bishops, and she wished her people to be gradually educated up to her conception. Much has been said about her contemptuous treatment of her Bishops. The celebrated letter to the Bishop of Ely, beginning: "Proud prelate," and ending: "by God, I will unfrock you," has long been known to be an amusing forgery; but it is still repeated, and is quoted as typical of her treatment of Bishops. As a matter of fact she treated them with greater respect than she showed to any of her ministers or favourites. Her position was one of watchful protection of the Church and its order.

Its framework was not to be altered, and she repelled all attempts in that direction; but within that framework things might settle themselves; she would leave all points of detail for free discussion. In Whitgift she found for the first time a man who was strong enough in his own opinions to wish to restrain the clergy within the limits of the formularies of the Church. She would not have him meddled with, though her ministers thought that his action was perilous. She stood alone in supporting him.

Whitgift's activity produced much discontent among the Puritan clergy, because it showed that they were not to be allowed to transform the Church from within. This knowledge led to the formation of a body of Separatists, whose tenets seem to have been first formulated by Robert Browne, who asserted that religion was not under the control of the civil magistrate, that the Church was a voluntary company of Christians, and that each congregation ought to determine its own worship and be ruled by its own elders. Some of Browne's followers went further and denounced the Church of England as being no true Church, asserting that its worship was "flat idolatry" and that none of its Bishops or preachers preached Christ truly. They were tried before the Court of High Commission and committed to prison. But, in 1588, when the Armada was threatening England, a number of pamphlets attacking the Bishops were secretly printed and issued under the name of "Martin Marprelate". They were at first answered seriously, but ultimately were left to men of letters such as Nash and Lilly, who retorted with a scurrility nearly as great as that of the Separatist writers. At first the public was amused at the display of trenchant style and hard hitting. But it was soon seen that this controversy was unworthy, and went beyond the limits of fair discussion. Public opinion turned against the Separatists: the old Puritan party refused to make common cause with them, and preferred to accept the liberty which the Church allowed them rather than embark on revolutionary projects. The Separatists fell upon the laws enacted against the Romanist recusants, which were applied to them with leniency, and were only directed against their leaders.

When Parliament met, in February, 1593, Elizabeth was resolved to keep it in due subjection on those points which she reserved for herself. She sent a message: "Mr. Speaker, Her Majesty's pleasure is, that if you perceive any idle heads, which will not stick to hazard their own estates, which will meddle with reforming the Church and transforming the commonwealth, and do exhibit any bills to such purpose, that you do not receive them until they be viewed and considered by those who it is fitter should consider of such things". Undeterred by this message, Peter Wentworth proposed that a joint committee of Lords and Commons should petition the Queen to settle the succession; he was committed to the Tower. A Puritan laywer, James Morice, introduced bills for the reformation of ecclesiastical courts and the revision of the penal statutes; he was arrested in the Queen's name and was sent to Tutbury Castle. An Act was passed, directly aimed at the Separatists, "to restrain the Queen's subjects in obedience". It provided that any one who refused to go to Church, or denied the Queen's authority in matters ecclesiastical, or frequented unlawful assemblies, should be imprisoned till he had made submission. Another Act was passed against Popish recusants, ordering them to repair to their place of dwelling and not to remove more than five miles from it, under pain of forfeiture. It would seem that England was wearied of religious conflict and was willing to resort to severe measures in the hopes of enforcing peace.

The unfortunate result of this legislation was the execution of some of the Nonconformist leaders, though proceedings were not taken on religious grounds. Barrow and Greenwood were found guilty of "defaming the Queen with malicious intent, to the stirring up of rebellion". Penry, who was the chief author of the Martin Marprelate tracts, was indicted for writing slanders with the intent to stir up rebellion, and the evidence was taken, not from published writings, but from papers found in his house. These executions were deplorable and unnecessary. Such sectaries might be troublesome, but it could not be said that they were disloyal, or tended to endanger the State. The example of such treatment led to the flight of many conscientious men to Holland, where they developed their opinions unchecked, and formed the body of Independents who were so powerful in the great Civil War.

It was one of the misfortunes of Elizabeth that she was never permitted for long to enjoy the feeling of personal security. A plot against her life was brought to light in 1594, about which it is difficult to form a correct judgment. Essex vied with Burghley in obtaining secret information from abroad, and used for this purpose a Portuguese Jew, Rodrigo Lopez, who had settled in London as a physician, and was employed by the Queen. He also welcomed into England a Spanish refugee, Antonio Perez, who had formerly been secretary to Philip, but had incurred his enmity. Spanish spies in London endeavoured to bribe some of Perez's servants to murder him and the Queen. Lopez was approached for the same purpose, and accepted some jewels as presents from Philip. The matter was discovered by Essex, but, at first, Burghley disbelieved it, and Elizabeth chided Essex as "a rash and temerarious youth to enter into a matter against a poor man which he could not prove". However, more evidence was obtained, and Lopez was incriminated, was tried and found guilty. For three months Elizabeth hesitated, but at last signed the warrant for his execution. It is most probable that the popular excitement about this trial directed Shakespeare's attention to the Jews, and that Lopez suggested the character of Shylock.

Elizabeth's parsimony is proverbial; but it must be admitted that it was thorough-going. She attached men to her at the smallest possible cost, and only rewarded those whom she wished for personal reasons to bind closely to herself. Leicester was wealthy while he lived, but after his death the Queen resumed her grants. Her chief ministers did not receive any great recompense at her hands, nor did her relatives. Nearest to her in blood was Henry Carey, only son of her mother's sister. He was created Baron Hunsdon, and was sent to guard the Scottish marches, where he rendered most valuable service. A bluff, outspoken soldier, he could be trusted entirely; and he was the father of seven sons who helped him in his government of the borders. Yet Hunsdon's salary was frequently in arrears, and he had to spend his own money for the payment of his forces. His youngest son, Robert, determined to try his fortunes as a courtier, and his description of his experience is typical of that of many others. "I lived in Court," he says, "had small means of my friends; yet God so blessed me that I was ever able to keep company with the best. In all triumphs I was one, either at tilt, tourney, or barriers, in masque or balls. I kept men and horses far above my rank, and so continued a long time." He served the Queen in many things, and once she gave him a thousand pounds to pay his debts. In 1593 he married a lady "more for her worth than for her wealth. Neither did she marry me for any great wealth; for I had in all the world but one hundred pounds a year pension out of the Exchequer, and that was but during pleasure, and I was near a thousand pounds in debt." The Queen was, as usual, indignant that any one should marry, while she had remained single, and Carey found it wise to retire with his wife to the border. After a time he made a bold attempt to win the Queen's forgiveness. He went to the festivities with which she celebrated her coronation day. "I prepared a present," he tells us, "for Her Majesty, which with my caparisons cost me about four hundred pounds. I came into the triumph unknown of any. I was the Forsaken Knight, that had vowed solitariness, but hearing of this great triumph thought to honour my mistress with my best services, and then return to pay my wonted mourning." But Elizabeth had no immediate need of Carey, and made no sign, till presently Lord Hunsdon informed her that the Scottish King wished to make a communication to her. "I hear," said the Queen, "that your fine son, that has lately married so worthily, is

hereabouts. Send him if you will, to know the King's pleasure."
Hunsdon answered that his son would be glad to obey her commands. "No," said she, "do you bid him go; for I have nothing to
do with him." Carey went, and James entrusted him with a
verbal message; but he dexterously said that he dared not trust his
memory and would prefer to have it in writing. When he returned to the Court he refused to deliver his message save to the
Queen herself. "With much ado I was called for in, and I was
left alone with her. Our first encounter was stormy and terrible,
which I passed over with silence. After she had spoken her pleasure of me and my wife I told her that she herself was the fault of
my marriage, and that if she had but graced me with the least of
her favours I had never left her nor her Court; and seeing she was
the chief cause of my misfortune I would never off my knees till
I had kissed her hand and obtained pardon. She was not displeased
with my excuse, and before we parted we grew good friends."

Such was the strange method by which Elizabeth held men in
dependence on herself. It may be ascribed to vanity, but as-
suredly it was also due to policy. The capricious bestowal and
withdrawal of favour kept men perpetually on the alert, sharp-
ened their wits, and provided a test of their dexterity. The
affectation of dislike to their marriages afforded a calculable
opportunity, when a man was still young, of trying his mettle. A
stormy scene, ending in a gracious reconciliation, gave Elizabeth
an occasion of displaying all her qualities alike as a woman and a
Queen. As time went on she took more pleasure in the process,
and found it increasingly necessary as a means of keeping young
bloods in due subjection.

Meanwhile, in foreign affairs, Elizabeth was content to keep
Spain at bay. The death of the Duke of Parma, in 1592, removed
Philip's great general, and Prince Maurice began a career of military skill which won the freedom of the United Netherlands.
Henry IV., in France, with Elizabeth's help, made head against
the league which was supported by Spain. But Henry saw that he
could never hope to unite France so long as he remained a

Huguenot, and, in the autumn of 1593, executed a politic change of his religion. Elizabeth addressed him with an angry remonstrance:—

"Ah, what grief! ah, what regret! ah, what pangs have seized my heart! My God, is it possible that any worldly considerations could render you regardless of the Divne displeasure? Can we reasonably expect any good result can follow such an iniquity? How can you imagine that He whose hand has supported and upheld your cause so long would fail you at your need? It is a perilous thing to do ill that good may come. Nevertheless I yet hope that your better feelings may return, and, in the meantime, I promise to give you the first place in my prayers, that Esau's hands may not defile the blessing of Jacob. Your sister, if it be after the old fashion; with the new, I will have nothing to do.

"E. R."

However, Henry's conversion was not at first recognised by the Pope and the King of Spain, and the war was still continued by the league. Henry drew nearer to England, and, in 1595, an alliance was made between him, England, and the United Netherlands, which were then recognised as a sovereign Power, for the purpose of waging war against Spain; but there was not much heart in the undertaking, for it was felt that Henry IV. was feeling his way towards peace. Even diplomacy was conducted in a fantastic fashion. Henry IV. protested to Sir Henry Unton that Elizabeth's letters were "full of sweetness and affection but that she could not escape from her ministers: so he for his part was obliged to do for the preservation of his subjects what as Henry her loving brother he would never do". Then he sent for his mistress, Gabrielle d'Estrées, and talked for an hour on frivolous topics. He afterwards led Unton into his chamber, "where in a private place between the bed and the wall he asked me how I liked his mistress. I answered sparingly in her praise, and told him that I had the picture of a far more excellent mistress, and yet did her picture come far short of the perfection of her beauty." When the King pressed for a sight of this picture, Unton produced a miniature of Elizabeth. Henry "beheld it with passion and admiration, saying that I had reason, that he had never seen the like; so with great reverence he kissed it twice or thrice, I detaining it still in my hand. In the end, with some kind of contention, he took it from me, vowing that he could not forego it for any treasure; and that to possess the favour of the lively picture he would forsake all the world, and hold himself most happy, with many other most passionate words." The style which Elizabeth had invented in England was now transplanted abroad. Hatton and Essex were outdone by the French King.

But although gallantry had invaded diplomacy, the martial spirit of England was stirred in March, 1596, by the news that the Archduke Charles had entered France and was laying siege to Calais. Levies were called out at once, but Calais fell before anything was done. Its possession by Spain was felt to be an important help to a new Armada, which was continually threatened; and Elizabeth was driven to depart from her pacific course. An expedition was fitted out against Spain. Lord Howard of Effingham was put in command of the fleet, and Essex in command of the land forces. They destroyed the Spanish fleet in Cadiz Bay, captured the town, and razed its fortifications. It was a crushing blow struck at the power of Spain and was more decisive than the defeat of the Armada.

But Elizabeth was not elated by glory; she was disappointed that no portion of the spoils reached her Exchequer. Cadiz had been given up to plunder, and every one took what he could get; there was no capture of treasure ships whose contents went to the Queen. News came that only two days after the departure of the English fleet, ships bearing twenty millions of ducats entered the Tagus. Great was Elizabeth's anger at this lost opportunity, and she disputed the right of those who had divided among themselves the ransom of Cadiz. When Burghley expressed his opinion in their favour he had to bear the burden of her displeasure, "with words," he wrote to Essex, "of indignity, reproach, and rejecting of me as a miscreant and a coward". Between the Queen and Essex, Burghley found it more difficult to steer in his old age than he had ever found it in the days of Leicester. The only thanks he received was the glee of the friends of Essex that he "had made the old fox to crouch and whine, and to insinuate himself by a very submissive letter to my Lord of Essex".

The position of Essex was remarkable. He was the idol of the younger party, and seemed to be the master of the future. For this reason he was regarded as dangerous by the more cautious of the Queen's advisers, notably Burghley. The permanent appointment of Robert Cecil as secretary established in Elizabeth's counsels a balance of opinion which enabled her to reserve her own freedom. But Essex was ever trying to assert himself, and to win a victory over those whom he regarded as his opponents. He regarded every appointment as an opportunity for a pitched battle. He put forward a candidate of his own, and strove desperately to force him upon the Queen. Elizabeth allowed him to plead for a long time, but ultimately rejected his recommendation. She was too prudent to allow any one to dispose of public offices and surround her by creatures of his own; and she took care to mark clearly the limits of Essex's influence. The wiser of his friends saw that he was following a mistaken course; they deplored his impetuosity, and tried to school him into some semblance of caution. In his private life he was continually irritating the Queen by love affairs with ladies of the Court, which Elizabeth bitterly resented, and often vented her displeasure on the luckless objects of Essex's pursuit. Amongst those who owed much to the goodwill of Essex, and hoped for more, was Francis Bacon, who admonished his patron in a letter full of wise saws of worldly wisdom, of a different tone to those contained in his *Essays*. With curious audacity Bacon wrote: "I said to your Lordship last time, 'Martha, Martha, attendis ad pluria, unum sufficit,' win the Queen. If this be not the beginning, of any other course I can see no end. But how is it now? A man of a nature not to be ruled, that hath my affection and knoweth it, of an estate not grounded to his greatness, of a popular reputation, of a military dependence: I demand whether there can be a more dangerous image than this represented to any monarch living, much more to a lady, and of Her Majesty's apprehension?" So Bacon advised Essex to apologise for his petulance in the past; to imitate Leicester and Hatton, and quote them "for authors and patterns" to the Queen; to show more cordiality in agreeing with the Queen's opinions; to make some requests to the Queen with the intention of withdrawing them "upon taking note of Her Majesty's opposition and dislike". Further, he must not be so war-like in his talk, "for Her Majesty loveth peace; next she loveth not change". Let him not seek military posts, but civil, such as Lord Privy Seal. Moreover, Essex must diminish the impression that he seeks popularity, by "speaking against popular courses vehemently, and taxing it in others, but nevertheless go on in your honourable commonwealth courses as you do". Bacon's cynicism regarded Elizabeth as easier to deceive, and Essex more responsive to advice, than either of them was; but his letter shows that a political career was recognised as a form of personal adven-ture, and that the principles on which it was founded were studied in England as carefully as they had been by Machiavelli in Italy.

Essex considered himself the most popular man in England, the special representative of the new national life. He dreamed of military glory, and was full of ambitious projects, which the Queen constantly restrained. But, at times, there was need for an armed demonstration to secure peace. There were rumours that Philip was preparing another Armada, and a large fleet was fitted out by England to ward off invasion. In the summer of 1597 it put to sea in three squadrons commanded by Essex, Raleigh, and Lord Thomas Howard. The weather was adverse, and little was achieved. Elizabeth was indignant, and vented her displeasure on Essex, who withdrew to his house at Wanstead. She further annoyed him by creating Lord Howard of Effingham, the Lord Admiral, Earl of Nottingham, and in so doing rehearsed his serv-ices in the defeat of the Armada, and also in the capture of Cadiz. Essex claimed for himself the glory of this last achievement, and was further aggrieved that Nottingham was made Lord Steward, and so took precedence over himself. The result was a quarrel between him and Nottingham, till at last the Queen for the sake of peace made Essex Earl Marshal, and so restored his precedence, whereupon Nottingham was discontented and left the Court. On all sides Elizabeth felt the increasing difficulty of maintaining her system of personal government against the growing spirit of independence which marked the revival of England. In spite of all her efforts her courtiers asserted their own position and escaped from the devices by which she tried to keep them in subjection to her will.

In 1598 the foreign policy of England was seriously affected by the peace which Henry IV. of France made with Spain. War with Spain, in alliance with France and the Netherlands, had been a normal state of things for ten years. As Spain could not invade England, war only meant that England made raids upon the Spanish ports and shipping whenever it was convenient to do so. It now became a question whether England should aim at dismembering the Spanish Empire or should follow the example of France and make peace on good terms. On this point there was a difference of opinion between the old politicians, such as Burghley, and the younger men, such as Essex and Raleigh. There was a warm debate in the Council, and Burghley was provoked by the outspoken urgency for warfare shown by Essex. He said that "he seemed intent on nothing but blood and slaughter". He took from his pocket a Prayer-Book, and with tremulous finger pointed to the words: "Men full of blood shall not live out half their days".

Essex prevailed so far as to prevent any negotiations for peace, and was elated at his success. His presumption grew till the Queen's patience was exhausted. One day, during a discussion about the appointment of a Lord Deputy for Ireland, Essex was irritated that Elizabeth did not follow his advice. He turned his back upon her with a gesture of contempt. Elizabeth's wrath flamed out in a moment. She gave Essex a box on the ear, and told him to "go and be hanged". Essex, in a fury, clutched his sword, and Nottingham had to come between them and drag away Essex, who swore that he would not have brooked such an affront from Henry VIII. himself. It was some time before Essex could be induced to apologise, but Elizabeth never entirely forgave him.

In July, 1598, Burghley lay on his deathbed, where Elizabeth frequently tended him. In a letter to his son the dying man wrote: "Serve God by serving the Queen, for all other service is indeed bondage to the devil". Such had been Burghley's maxim during his long life; and Elizabeth recognised his fidelity. She said "that her comfort had been in her people's happiness, and their happiness in his discretion". It was long before she could hear his name without shedding tears. The same year that saw Elizabeth deprived of her trusty minister saw also the removal of her great opponent, Philip II. An epoch was closed, and Elizabeth still lived on, growing old and feeble in a rapidly changing world, which had outgrown her methods, and was looking forward to a new future.

VIII

LAST YEARS OF
ELIZABETH

~§ We have a description of Elizabeth in 1598 from the pen
of a German traveller, which tells us minutely how the burden of
her years did not diminish her taste for splendour. On a Sunday in
September he saw the Queen going to chapel at her palace of
Greenwich. "The presence-chamber was richly hung with tapes-
try and strewn with rushes. In it were assembled the Archbishop
of Canterbury, the Bishop of London, and the chief officers of
the Crown. The Queen appeared, preceded by gentlemen,
barons, earls, knights of the Garter, all richly dressed and bare-
headed. Next came the Lord High Chancellor, bearing the seals in
a red silk purse, between two, one of whom carried the royal
sceptre, the other the sword of State in a red scabbard. Next
came the Queen, very majestic; her face oblong, fair but wrin-
kled; her eyes small, yet black and pleasant; her nose a little
hooked, her lips narrow, and her teeth black (a defect the English
seem subject to from their too great use of sugar). She had in her
ears two pearls with very rich drops; her hair was of an auburn
colour, but false; upon her head she had a small crown; her
bosom was uncovered, as all the English ladies have it till they
marry; and she had on a necklace of exceedingly fine jewels. Her
hands were slender, her fingers rather long, and her stature neither tall nor low. Her air was stately, and her manner of speech
gracious. She was dressed in white silk, bordered with pearls of
the size of beans, and over it a mantle of black silk shot with silver threads; her train was very long, the end of it borne by a
marchioness. Instead of a chain she had an oblong collar of gold

and jewels. As she went along in all this state and magnificence she spoke very graciously to foreign ministers or others, in English, French and Italian. Whosoever speaks to her kneels; now and then she raises some one with her hand. Wherever she turned her face, as she was going along, every one fell on their knees. The ladies of the Court followed her, very handsome and well-shaped, for the most part dressed in white. She was guarded on each side by the gentlemen-pensioners, fifty in number, with gilt halberds. In the ante-chapel petitions were presented to her, and she received them graciously, which occasioned the exclamation: 'God save Elizabeth!' She answered: 'I thank you, my good people'.

"While she was at prayers we saw her table set with the following solemnity: A gentleman entered bearing a rod, and along with him another who bore a table-cloth, which, after they had both knelt three times with the utmost veneration, he spread upon the table, and, after kneeling again, they both retired. Then came two others, one with a rod, the other with a salt-cellar, a plate and bread; they knelt, placed them on the table with the same ceremonies, and retired. Then came two ladies, one bearing a knife; one of them dressed in white silk, after kneeling three times, approached the table and rubbed the plate with bread and salt. The Yeomen of the Guard, clothed in scarlet, with a golden rose on their backs, brought in a course of twenty-four dishes, served in silver, mostly gilt. The dishes were received by a gentleman, who placed them on the table, while the lady taster gave to each of the guard a mouthful to eat of the dish which he carried, for fear of poison. During this time twelve trumpets and two kettle-drums made the hall ring. At the end of this ceremony a number of ladies appeared, who with particular ceremony lifted the meat from the table and carried it into the Queen's private chamber, where after she has chosen for herself, the rest goes to the ladies of the Court."

It would seem from this account that, as years went on, Elizabeth fenced herself round with greater state, and by an increase of magnificence in apparel tried to hide from herself and others the ravages of time. Certainly she objected to any reference to her age. When the Bishop of St. Davids preached a sermon on the text: "Lord teach us to number our days that we may apply our hearts unto wisdom," Elizabeth, instead of thanking him, according to her custom, told him that "he might have kept his arithmetic for himself; but I see that the greatest clerks are not the wisest men".

However much Elizabeth might long to end her days in all the glory of undisputed power, surrounded by the admiration of her Court and the love of her people, such was not to be her fortune. The last years of her reign were a series of reminders that her old supremacy had passed away. Difficulties arose and had to be faced; but though the decision still rested with herself, the advice which she needed was no longer couched in the old terms of dutiful submission. In August, 1598, Ireland had become a cause of serious alarm. The Irish had found a leader in Hugh O'Neill, who had been educated in England, and received from Elizabeth the Earldom of Tyrone. He was by education and habits an Englishman; but he was offered by the Irish the position of Lord of Tyrone, instead of his English earldom, and he aspired to become the O'Neill, and Lord of Ireland. He made himself the head of a national league against England, and cautiously waited till either help came from Spain or Elizabeth was wearied into recognition of his power. At last he defeated the English forces at Blackwater, and all the Celtic population gathered round him. It was necessary that active steps should be taken to put down the rebellion, and Elizabeth resolved to send an army of 16,000 men. There was a discussion who should be placed in command of the forces. It is said that Essex objected to those who were suggested by others, till, at last, the post was forced upon himself somewhat against his will. It was indeed a dangerous post to fill; and all foresaw that, in the case of Essex, failure would mean ruin.

If the expedition had been one which could be decided by some daring act of valour, Essex might have succeeded; but he

was incapable of dealing with the problem which Ireland presented. He squandered his forces on small undertakings, and incurred the Queen's displeasure in many matters of detail. When
his forces had been so reduced by sickness that he could not
fight, he held a conference with Tyrone and discussed conditions
of peace. Elizabeth angrily disavowed his action; whereupon
Essex, already thoroughly disheartened, hastily left Ireland, and
did not pause till he rushed into the Queen's presence at Non-
such. It was ten o'clock in the morning. Elizabeth had newly
risen, and was in the hands of her maid, "her hair about her face,"
when Essex burst into the room, his dress and face all covered
with mire, and began his excuses. At first he hoped that they
were accepted, and thought that "though he had suffered much
trouble and storms abroad he found a sweet calm at home". In
the afternoon he was disabused of his hopes. Elizabeth told him
that the Council would hear his explanation; he was ordered to
keep to his room. The charges against him were disobedience in returning from Ireland, presumptuous letters written to the Queen,
acting contrary to instructions, especially in making so many
knights, and finally his overbold intrusion into the Queen's bed-
chamber on his return. He was committed to the care of the
Lord Keeper and was not allowed to see the Queen.

Elizabeth nursed her wrath, and everything she heard from
Ireland confirmed it. Amongst those who had gone out with
Essex was John Harrington, a godson of the Queen, a wit and a
poet, whose chief contribution towards the pacification of Ireland had been the presentation of a copy of his translation of
Ariosto to Tyrone's son. He was one of the large number of
knights whom Essex had made contrary to the Queen's orders.
Harrington has left an account of his reception by Elizabeth;
though it was written seven years afterwards, he says: "Even
now I almost tremble to rehearse Her Highness's displeasure. She
chafed much, walked fastly to and fro, looked with discomposure
in her visage; and, I remember, she catched my girdle when I
kneeled to her, and swore 'By God's Son, I am no Queen. That

man is above me. Who gave him command to come here so soon? I did send him on other business.' It was long before more gracious discourse did fill my hearing, but I was then put out of my trouble and bid go home. I did not stay to be bidden twice; if all the Irish rebels had been at my heels I should not have made better speed, for I did now flee from one whom I both loved and feared too." Harrington had kept a journal of his doings in Ireland, which Elizabeth asked for. When she read it her wrath broke out again. "She swore by God's Son we were all idle knaves, and the Lord Deputy worse, for wasting our time and her commands in such wise as my journal doth write of." Finally Harrington was dismissed to his country house, with a deep impression on his mind. "Until I come to heaven I shall never come before a statelier judge again, nor one that can temper majesty, wisdom, learning, choler and favour better than Her Highness did at that time."

The more Elizabeth brooded over the conduct of Essex, the more deeply she resented it. He had disregarded her orders; he had acted as if he had independent authority; he had presumed upon her personal favour in a way which was marked and notorious. Elizabeth's plan of keeping young England in the same subjection as the older England, by attaching its leaders to herself, had entirely broken down, and she deeply resented the failure. The knowledge that Essex was popular, that men blamed her severity, that her Council advised that his release would be politic, were only tokens of her failure and deepened her resentment. As usual she hesitated and took no step until the public feeling had subsided. She showed herself more frequently in public, and took an unwonted part in festivities. "Almost every night, at Christmas time," we are told, "Her Majesty is in presence to see the ladies dance with tabour and pipe." In the beginning of 1600 she consulted Francis Bacon, whose capacities she was now beginning to understand, though she had refused to favour him on the recommendation of Essex, who had compensated him for his disappointment by a substantial present. Bacon was not successful in

displaying his gratitude. When he found that Elizabeth was resolved on the trial of Essex he was one of the counsel who pleaded
against him. In June Essex was brought before a Special Commission, which sentenced him to be deprived of all his offices and to
remain a prisoner in his own house at the Queen's pleasure. By
the end of August he was restored to liberty, but was forbidden
to come to Court.

Essex trusted that this prohibition would soon be removed, and
that he would be restored to favour. He wrote Elizabeth letters,
of which the briefest may serve as a sample:—

"Haste paper to that happy presence, whence only unhappy I am
banished. Kiss that fair correcting hand which lays new plasters to my
lighter hurts, but to my greatest wound applieth nothing. Say thou
comest from pining, languishing, despairing

"ESSEX."

He even compared himself to Nebuchadnezzar, content "to
eat grass like an ox, and be wet with the dew of heaven, till it
shall please Her Majesty to restore me to my understanding". But
Elizabeth had lost all confidence in his understanding, and was
minded to make him an example which would check all presumption in the future. Men should see that whom she made she could
likewise unmake, and that obedience was the paramount claim to
her favour. She was in no hurry to point this moral, but used opportunities as they came. At Michaelmas the monopoly of the im-
portation of sweet wines which had been granted to Essex on
Leicester's death expired and he applied for its renewal. Elizabeth
at first scornfully said that his dutiful letters had only been written to prepare the way for this request. Then she said that "she
must learn the value of it, as benefits were not conferred at ran-
dom". Finally she granted the monopoly to others, saying: "An
ungovernable beast must be stinted of his provender that he may
be better managed".

Essex was no statesman, and had no policy; but he had come
to regard himself as necessary to the Queen and to the country.
He could not accept the fact that his opportunity was lost by his

own folly; he persuaded himself that it was owing to sinister intrigues. He lost all self-control; "he shifteth," wrote Harrington, "from sorrow and repentance to rage and rebellion so suddenly as well proveth him devoid of good reason as of right mind. His speeches about the Queen become no man who has 'mens sana in corpore sano'." Unfortunately he was surrounded by friends who were as reckless as himself, men whose fortunes depended on his and who were ready to make a struggle for his restoration. When he left Ireland, Essex had thought of bringing with him some of his troops and making a demonstration of his power; now he reverted to the plan. A little pressure might secure the removal of the Queen's counsellors who were opposed to him, and bring him back to pre-eminence. The Scottish King was anxious to be recognised as Elizabeth's successor; he might make a demonstration for that purpose on the Border, and Essex would support him in England. Lord Mountjoy, who had succeeded Essex in Ireland, might detach some of his troops to help. Such like schemes were discussed by Essex and his friends, till they resolved that the one important thing was that Essex should have access to the Queen. In January, 1601, a plan was formed for seizing Whitehall; then Essex would approach the Queen with a request that his enemies should be dismissed from her Council, and a Parliament be summoned. The occasion was to be given by the arrival of ambassadors from Scotland, with whom Essex was to cooperate.

The stir at Essex House had been so great that the Government were well aware of all that was happening. Essex was summoned before the Council; whereupon it was hastily determined that a rising should be made at once. Essex, believing himself to be beloved by the Londoners, prepared to call them to his aid and with their help make his way into the Queen's presence. His friends gathered round him to the number of 300 men, and, on the morning of Sunday, February 8, the Lord Keeper, the Lord Chief Justice and others went to Essex House to ask the meaning of this concourse. Essex passionately shouted out that there was a plot to murder him in his bed; and he was there to defend his life. When they would have expostulated further there was a confused uproar; they were taken to a room where they were kept prisoners. Essex, with his followers, hurried towards the City, crying out: "For the Queen! for the Queen! a plot is laid against my life". The people looked on in silent amazement. Meanwhile proclamation was made in various parts of the city that Essex and his men were traitors. It was impossible for him to make his way to the Queen; he managed to reach the river and return home by boat. There he found that the Lord Keeper and his fellow-prisoners had been allowed to escape. Soon the house was besieged, and Essex surrendered.

Elizabeth heard the noise of this tumult, but was undisturbed. She spoke of going forth to meet the rebels, saying that "not one of them would dare to meet a single glance of her eye". She soon heard that there was no need for her presence. Indeed the rising had no prospect of success; it had no intelligible object, and appealed to nothing in men's minds: it was an outburst of childish vanity. Elizabeth issued a proclamation thanking the citizens for their loyalty. A Commission was soon appointed to try Essex and his friend Southampton. The trial showed the readiness of all concerned to throw the blame on one another, and much time was spent in mutual recriminations. Essex accused Sir Robert Cecil of maintaining the right of the Infanta of Spain to the English succession, a charge which Cecil denied on his knees. When Raleigh was called, Essex exclaimed: "What booteth it to swear this fox?" Francis Bacon, remembering only too well his former relations to Essex, strove to shake them off by the bitterness of his pleading till Essex said that he should like "to call Bacon to witness against Bacon the pleader". The proceedings were a miserable exhibition of personal motives and selfish intrigue. Essex was condemned to death as a traitor. At first Elizabeth hesitated to sign the warrant for his execution. At last she did so, and on February 25 the head of Essex fell upon the the scaffold.

This was the dismal end of Elizabeth's plan of retaining the allegiance of her subjects by their affections. The Tudor rule, it seemed, could never be free from the scaffold. The reign that had begun with all the difficulties of a disputed succession ended with like difficulties. Elizabeth wished to end her days in undisputed splendour: those around her were looking to the future, and were scheming for their own advancement when the change came. This knowledge embittered Elizabeth's last days, but did not tame her courage. She would be true to herself to the end. In the autumn she went on a progress to Hampshire, where she was entertained by the Marquess of Winchester at Basing. There she received an embassy from Henry IV., headed by the Duc de Biron, and took care to impress her guests by her stateliness. She had the satisfaction of thinking she had done what no other Prince could do; she had royally entertained an ambassador in the houses of her subjects.

In October Elizabeth summoned her last Parliament, and at its opening showed signs of fatigue. It was remarkable for an outspoken debate against monopolies, grants of the sole right to sell various articles—so numerous that when they were rehearsed a member sarcastically asked: "Is not bread there?" Another answered: "If order be not taken, bread will be there before next Parliament". Such grants were Elizabeth's economical method of rewarding her officers and favourites, and were naturally found to be oppressive. Francis Bacon said all that could be said in their favour; but Elizabeth saw that it was necessary to give way, and, summoning the Speaker, told him that she had lately become aware that "divers patents, which she had granted, were grievous to her subjects"; she had had the matter in mind "before the late trouble," and since then, "even in the midst of her most great and weighty occasions, she thought upon them"; she promised immediate reform. The Commons sent a deputation to thank her, which assured her that no words would be sufficient for so great goodness, "but in all duty and thankfulness, prostrate at your feet, we present our most loyal and thankful hearts, and the last spirit in our nostrils, to be poured out, to be breathed up, for your safety".

Elizabeth used the opportunity to proclaim with dignity the principles on which she reigned. The Commons knelt as she addressed them: "There is no jewel, be it of never so rich a price, which I prefer before this jewel, I mean your love. For I do more esteem it than any treasure or riches; for that we know how to prize, but love and thanks I count inestimable. And though God hath raised me high, yet this I count the glory of my Crown, that I have reigned with your loves. This makes that I do not so much rejoice that God hath made me a Queen, as to be Queen over so thankful a people." Her only object was to promote the prosperity of her people. She never wished for money, except for her subjects' good; she asked for nothing from them for her own use, but spent her own in their service. Then she paused and bade them stand up as she had more to say. She thanked the House for bringing their grievances to her knowledge, as otherwise she might have erred through lack of information. She had never made any grant, except in the belief that it was beneficial; she was glad to know if experience proved it to be otherwise. She regretted that she had been deceived by those who ought to have advised her better. "I have ever used to set the Last Judgment Day before my eyes, and so to rule as I shall be judged to answer before a higher Judge, to whose judgment seat I do appeal that never thought was cherished in my heart that tended not to my people's good. To be a King and wear a crown is more glorious to them that see it than it is pleasure to them that bear it. For myself I was never so much enticed with the glorious name of a King, or royal authority of a Queen, as delighted that God hath made me the instrument to maintain His truth and glory, and to defend the kingdom from peril, dishonour, tyranny and oppression. There will never Queen sit in my seat with more zeal to my country, or care to my subjects, that will sooner with willingness yield and venture her life for your good and safety than myself.

And though you have had, and may have, many Princes more mighty and wise sitting in this seat, yet you never had, nor shall have, any that will be more careful and loving. I speak it to give God the praise as a testimony before you, and not to attribute anything to myself. For I, O Lord what am I whom practices and perils past should not fear? O what can I do that I should speak for any glory? God forbid." She raised her voice and spoke these last words with marked emphasis; then she dismissed the members, bidding them all to kiss her hand before they departed.

It was Elizabeth's last great triumph. Clouds passed away, and she stood forth again as the mother of her people, whose heart beat with theirs, and whose ear was open to their petitions. If she erred, it was in ignorance; when they spoke of wrongs, she was ready to give redress. In her Court she might be surrounded by intrigue, and her efforts to restrain her nobles might end in failure; but she could pierce through her surroundings and meet her people face to face, and count on her hold upon their affections. At the end of the year she heard the news that victory had crowned her arms in Ireland, where Mountjoy won a decisive victory over Tyrone and his Spanish helpers. She could look around proudly with the feeling that again her difficulties had disappeared.

Age did not abate Elizabeth's activity, and those who were around her wondered at her vigour. In April, 1602, she entertained the Duc de Nevers and opened a ball with him. On May Day she went a-maying in the woods of Lewisham. She gave the Scottish King a hint that he need not be eager for her succession, by keeping his ambassador waiting in a passage where he could see her dancing in her chamber. In the summer she paid several visits according to her wont. Nor did her spirits fail, but still she could play tricks on her ministers, and make fun of Robert Cecil, who tried to pay his court to her with awkward gallantry. She saw the Countess of Derby wearing a picture round her neck and asked to see it. Lady Derby tried to keep it from her, which increased the Queen's curiosity. When the gold case was opened it proved to contain a portrait of Cecil, who was Lady Derby's uncle. The Queen, to hide her disappointment, tied the picture to her shoe and walked away with it. Then she fastened it to her elbow and wore it for some time. Cecil wrote a poem on this occurrence, and had it set to music and sung to the Queen. Its point was that he was content with the favours which he had received, and did not repine at the good fortune of others. In September the Earl of Worcester wrote: "We are frolic here in Court; much dancing in the Privy Chamber of country dances before the Queen's Majesty, who is exceedingly pleased therewith. Irish tunes are at this time most pleasing; but in winter, 'Lullaby,' an old song of Mr. Bird's, will be in most request, as I think." His prophecy proved true, for in the winter Elizabeth's health began to fail. At the end of the year Sir John Harrington wrote to his wife:—

"Our dear Queen, my royal godmother, and this State's natural mother, doth now bear show of human infirmity, too fast for that evil which we shall get by her death, and too slow for that good which we shall get by her releasement from pain and misery. It was not many days since I was bidden to her presence. I blessed the happy moment, and found in her a most pitiable state. She bade the Archbishop ask me if I had seen Tyrone. I replied with reverence that I had seen him with my Lord Deputy (Essex). She looked up with much choler and grief in her countenance, and said: 'Oh, now it mindeth me that you were one who saw this man elsewhere,' and hereat she dropped a tear and smote her bosom. She held in her hand a golden cup which she often put to her lips; but in sooth her heart seemeth too full to lack more filling. She bade me come to the chamber at seven o'clock, when she inquired of some matters which I had written; and as she was pleased to note my fanciful brain, I was not unheedful to feed her humour and read some verses, whereat she smiled once, and was pleased to say: 'When thou dost feel creeping time at thy gate, these fooleries will please thee less. I am past my relish for such matters. Thou seest my bodily meat doth not suit me well; I have eaten but one ill-tasted cake since yester-night.' She rated most grievously at noon at some who minded not to bring certain matters of account. Several men had been sent to, and when ready at hand, Her Highness hath dismissed them in anger. But who, dearest Moll, shall say that Her Highness hath forgotten?"

In January she somewhat recovered, and attended one or two state dinners; but, in the middle of the month, removed to Richmond by the advice of her physician. The change of air was at first beneficial, but soon there was a relapse. We have a pathetic account of the Queen's illness by her kinsman, Robert Carey. "When I came to the Court I found the Queen ill-disposed, and she kept her inner lodging; yet she hearing of my arrival sent for me. I found her in one of her withdrawing chambers, sitting low upon her cushions. She called me to her; I kissed her hand and told her it was my chiefest happiness to see her in safety and in health, which I wished might long continue. She took me by the hand, and wrung it hard, and said: 'No, Robin, I am not well,' and then discoursed with me of her indisposition, and that her heart had been sad and heavy for ten or twelve days, and in her discourse she fetched not so few as forty or fifty great sighs. I was grieved at the first to see her in such plight; for in all my lifetime before I never knew her fetch a sigh but when the Queen of Scots was beheaded. Then, upon my knowledge, she shed many tears and sighs, manifesting her innocence that she never gave consent to the death of that Queen. I used the best words I could to persuade her from this melancholy humour; but I found it was too deeply rooted in her heart, and hardly to be removed. This was upon a Saturday night, and she gave command that the great closet should be prepared for her to go to chapel the next morning. The next day, all things being in readiness, we long expected her coming. After eleven o'clock one of the grooms came out and bade make ready for the private closet; she would not go to the great. There we stayed long for her coming; but, at last, she had cushions laid for her in the Privy Chamber, hard by the closet door, and there she heard service. From that day forwards she grew worse and worse. She remained upon her cushions four days and nights at the least. All about her could not persuade her either to take sustenance or go to bed."

At length Nottingham and Cecil tried to persuade her, and Cecil said that "to content the people she must go to bed". Elizabeth recovered her spirit and said: "The word *must* was not used to Princes. Little man, little man, if your father had lived you durst not have said so much, but you know I must die, and that makes you presumptuous." She was with difficulty induced to take to her bed, and the Council remained at Richmond awaiting the end. They were anxious for some expression of her wishes about the succession. Before leaving Whitehall she had said to Nottingham that "her throne had always been the throne of Kings, and none but her next heir of blood and descent should succeed. On March 22, Nottingham, in the presence of others, reminded her of her words and asked her pleasure. "I told you," said Elizabeth, "my seat had been the seat of Kings, and I will have no rascal to succeed me; who should succeed me but a King?" Cecil inquired her meaning "no rascal shall succeed". She answered: "My meaning was a King should succeed me; and who should that be but our cousin of Scotland?" On March 23 she was speechless, and when Cecil asked her to confirm her wishes about the succession she was supposed to have made a sign of assent when the Scottish King was mentioned.

"About six at night," says Carey, "she made signs for the Archbishop and her chaplains to come to her, at which time I went in with them and fell upon my knees, full of tears to see the heavy sight. Her Majesty lay upon her back, with one hand in the bed, and the other without. The Archbishop knelt down by her, and examined her first of her faith, and she so punctually answered all his several questions, by lifting up her eyes and holding up her hand, as it was a great comfort to all the beholders. Then the good man told her plainly what she was, and what she was to come to; and though she had been long a great Queen here upon earth, yet shortly she was to yield an account of her stewardship to the King of kings. After this he began to pray, and all that were by did answer him. After he had continued long in prayer, till the old man's knees were weary, he blessed her and meant to rise and leave her. The Queen made a sign with her hand. My Sister Scroope, knowing her meaning, told the Archbishop the Queen desired he would pray still. He did so for a long half-hour after, and then thought to leave her. The second time she made a sign to have him continue in prayer. He did so for half an hour more, with earnest cries to God for her soul's health, which he uttered with that fervency of spirit, as the Queen to all our sight much rejoiced thereat, and gave testimony to us all of her Christian and comfortable end. By this time it grew late, and every one departed, all but her women that attended her."

After this Elizabeth sank into a deep sleep from which she never awakened. At three o'clock in the morning of March 24 it was found that her spirit had passed away. A few hours later Robert Carey was riding hard along the North road that he might be the first to bring to James the tidings that there was no one to oppose his accession to the English Crown.

The character of Elizabeth is difficult to detach from her actions. She represented England as no other ruler ever did. For the greater part of her long reign the fortunes of England absolutely depended upon her life, and not only the fortunes of England, but those of Europe as well. If England had passed under the Papal sway it is hard to see how Protestantism could have survived the repressive forces to which it would have been exposed. There were times when Elizabeth doubted if this could be avoided, times when any one, save Anne Boleyn's daughter, would have been tempted to make terms. In asking England to rally round her Elizabeth knew that she could not demand any great sacrifices on her behalf. By cultivating personal loyalty, by demanding it in exaggerated forms, she was not merely feeding

her personal vanity; she was creating a habit which was necessary
for the maintenance of her government. By avoiding risky undertakings, by keeping down public expense, she was not merely indulging her tendency to parsimony; she was warding off from
her people demands which they were unequal at that time to sus-
tain.

Elizabeth's imperishable claim to greatness lies in her instinctive sympathy with her people. She felt, rather than understood,
the possibilities which lay before England, and she set herself the
task of slowly exhibiting, and impressing them on the national
mind. She educated Englishmen to a perception of England's destiny, and for this purpose fixed England's attention upon itself.
She caught at every advantage which was afforded by the divided
condition of Europe to assert England's importance. France and
Spain alike had deep causes of hostility; she played off one against
the other, so that both were anxious for the friendship of a State
which they each hoped some day to annex. England gained courage from this sight and grew in self-confidence. To obtain this
result Elizabeth was careless of personal dignity or honour. She
did not care how her conduct was judged at the time, but
awaited the result.

It is this faculty of intuitive sympathy with her people which
makes Elizabeth so difficult to understand in details of her policy.
The fact was that she never faced a question in the shape in
which it presented itself. It was true that it had to be recognised
and discussed in that form; but Elizabeth had no belief in a policy
because it could be clearly stated and promised well. Things had
to be discussed, and decisions arrived at in consequence of such
discussion; but action could always be avoided at the last
moment, and Elizabeth would never act unless she felt that her
people were in hearty agreement with her. Thus in her position
towards her ministers she represented in her own person the
vacillations and fluctuations of popular opinion. Ministers naturally wish to have an intelligible policy. Burghley laboriously

drew up papers which balanced the advantages and disadvantages of alternative courses of action. Elizabeth read them and seemed to accept one out of two inevitable plans. She felt that, as a reasonable being, she could not do otherwise. But when it came to decisive action she fell back upon her instinctive perception of what England wanted. As she could not explain this, she was driven to all sorts of devices to gain time. She could not, on the other hand, fully take her people into her confidence. It was the unconscious tendency of their capacities which she interpreted, not their actual demands. She was eliciting from them their meaning, and educating them to understand it themselves. For this purpose she must seem to govern more absolutely than she did; but, on great occasions, she took them into her confidence, and fired them with a high conception of the greatness of their national life. She strove to focus and co-ordinate all their aspirations, and only repressed tendencies which were adverse to the formation of an English spirit; for she cared more for the spirit of the national life than for its outward organisation.

Her private character is hard to detach from her public character. She behaved to those around her as she did to her people in general. She was surrounded by men representative of English life; they must be made to fall into line; and any method which served this purpose was good. Above all things she must impose her will equally on all. Personally, she was attracted by physical endowments, and let herself go in accordance with her feelings up to a certain point. But she was both intellectually and emotionally cold. In politics and in private life alike she cared little for decorum, because she knew that she could stop short whenever prudence made it needful.

It is easy to point out serious faults in Elizabeth, to draw out her inconsistencies, and define her character in a series of paradoxes. But this treatment does not exhibit the real woman, still less the real Queen. Elizabeth was hailed at her accession as being "mere English"; and "mere English" she remained. Round her, with all her faults, the England which we know grew into the consciousness of its destiny. The process was difficult; the struggle was painful, and it left many scars behind. There are many things in Elizabeth which we could have wished otherwise; but she saw what England might become, and nursed it into the knowledge of its power.